Another Vintage Book by June Fleming

The Well-fed Backpacker

Staying Found

Staying Found

The Complete Map and Compass Handbook

BY JUNE FLEMING

ILLUSTRATIONS BY WENDY WALLIN

VINTAGE BOOKS
A DIVISION OF RANDOM HOUSE
NEW YORK

A Vintage Original, April 1982

Copyright © 1982 by June Fleming

All rights reserved under International and Pan-American
Copyright Conventions. Published in the United States by Random
House, Inc., New York, and simultaneously in Canada by
Random House of Canada Limited, Toronto.

Grateful acknowledgment is made to the following for permission
to reprint previously published material:
United Feature Syndicate, Inc.: 11/14/80 PEANUTS cartoon
© 1980 United Feature Syndicate, Inc.

The author and the publisher wish to thank the U.S.
Geological Survey for the maps included in this book.

Library of Congress Cataloging in Publication Data
Fleming, June.
Staying found.
1. Orientation.   2. Wilderness survival.
I. Wallin, Wendy.   II. Title.
GV200.4.F55 1982   613.6'9   81–52429
ISBN 0–394–75152–3   AACR2

Manufactured in the United States of America
9876543

Designed by Naomi Osnos

Contents

Staying Found

1
Taking Off

Getting where you want to go with the help of map and compass is sometimes called orienteering. Various activities rely on these basic skills, from competitive meets on a charted course to the wilderness wanderings of a solitary backpacker. **The goal of this book is to show hikers, backpackers and other outdoor roamers how to make practical use of orienteering skills in their travels.** It deals with situations and problems they are likely to encounter, and provides answers to their particular route-finding needs.

Late at night the tent glows. Heads bend over a map, planning the next day's itinerary. A nameless small lake about two miles off the trail looks intriguing. A bearing from camp to the lake is plotted, then inch by inch the squiggly lines, colors and symbols of the map are deciphered and a likely cross-country route laid out.

I know this compass is broken! Everything's turned around. Some help!

Sam and Sal find a lovely meadow about a half-mile off the main trail. An unmaintained, overgrown trail leads to the clearing, but one could easily pass its junction with the main trail. They want to be sure they can find the takeoff point again.

The hiking friends reach Buck Prairie in the late afternoon. Tents are soon popping up in a circle, doors toward the hub. But there's Carrie, fiddling with her compass in the direction of the setting sun. She's figuring out where the sun will make its morning appearance so she can position her tent to catch the first warming rays.

Wandering away from camp with bird book and binoculars, Neil is engrossed in traipsing after some red-shafted flickers. Suddenly it hits—he isn't sure which way leads back to home base.

Jed had a vague recollection . . . something about the compass needle not really pointing north. "Wish I'd got that down pat. Well, I'll just have to ignore it and hike the way the map shows. It's only a mile cross-country." A couple of hours later Jed is stumbling around in a mild panic, a quarter-mile off his destination.

Dan is badly hurt. Someone needs to go out for help. Although the ridges enclosing the valley are rugged, there's one easy way over

—the notch his party came across the day before. But in the fog no one can see the notch.

Have you ever been in situations like these? They represent just a few of the reasons for mastering the skills of wilderness route-finding—the use of map and compass, and countless additional techniques for getting where you want to go in the backcountry and staying found.

Staying found is adequate reason in itself for *really* learning how to get around in the wild. Not just *carrying* a map and compass because they're on every book's list of essential items, but being *absolutely sure* how to use them to fullest advantage. Each year countless tragedies occur when people get lost in country and situations where they could have stayed found. Many hikers don't know *how* to stay found and, once lost, unwittingly compound their problems and work against being rescued. When searchers eventually locate a lost hiker, alive or dead, he sometimes has with him a compass he never learned to use.

Even if you choose to stick to trails, as a skilled route-finder you'll always know where you are and what you're looking at. You'll gain a feel for the wider landscape beyond the well-worn path. Knowing you aren't dependent on trails and signs will increase your confidence. Relaxed, you'll see more.

With map and compass as friends, you can explore beyond the tiny portion of the wilderness used by those who restrict their travels to popular trails and camps. Your paths and campsites will be pristine, quiet and private, even on a summer holiday weekend.

A map will become a vivid picture of the land whether you've been to the area or not. Studying it, you can plan trips to suit your needs, see what you want, challenge your abilities to become part of the country and give your body the kind of workout it's ready for.

With this knowledge, your chances of getting seriously lost are minimized. And when the day comes that you are temporarily "disoriented"—and it will, if you spend much time in far places—you'll be better able to summon up your resources and see the experience through to a happy conclusion.

Not the least of the benefits to be gained from your efforts is the satisfaction of learning a new and very practical set of skills. Map language, the turns of the compass, a feel for the lay of the land will add excitement to your travels as they push back the horizons for you.

Since the payoffs are so great, why doesn't every outdoor person learn route-finding skills? Why do many hikers feel confident with a topographic map but stop short of the compass?

Like many others, I was intimidated by the methods most often used to teach map and compass skills. They included too many formulas to remember, too many separate parts that I couldn't assemble into a useful, orderly whole.

As my outdoor ventures multiplied over the years, the need for way-finding skills grew. Eventually I took those parts of each method which were easiest for me to use, and from them worked out a sensible, easily remembered map and compass procedure. All procedures start from the same point—one that is easy to learn, and that incorporates the necessary adjustments.

With this unified system it's much easier to understand *what* you're doing and *why*, and consequently, *how* to do it. In the classes I've been teaching for years (back-packing, snow camping, wilderness route-finding) it's been gratifying to see face after face light up with "*Now* I understand it!" and know that map and compass work has been demystified for the students. It has taken a place in their stock of accessible, useful skills for outdoor safety and pleasure.

There are many types of compasses and many ways of doing map and compass procedures; other books treat these options thoroughly. My intention is not to review them all, but to give a clear presentation of the system I've found easiest to learn, apply and teach, using the kind of compass I consider most practical for hikers. This is the "orienteering" compass, with a transparent base plate attached to the compass housing. Models made by two Swedish companies, Silva and Suunto, are available at most outdoor stores.

This book is arranged to guide you through use of the basic tools and skills in a way that will be immediately helpful. After an overview are chapters devoted to the fundamentals of maps, compass use and the procedures in which both are used together. "True Directions" teaches how to measure directions in a way that's useful for certain special purposes. "Looking to Nature for Help" shows how the sun and stars, for example, give clues about direction and time. Laying out an excursion either on or off trails is the subject of "Route Planning."

Once you get out there, what can you do with all this? "How to Stay Found" discusses the dozens of things a hiker can do to get where he wants to go and to know where he is; it also explains what to do if plans go awry despite his best efforts and he gets lost. "Teaching Kids to Stay Found" presents a whole raft of specific ways to help children develop route-finding skills.

Many people put away their boots come fall and hole up till the spring thaw. But for those wanderers whose appetites are whetted anew by the first snowfall, there's "Route-finding on Snow." This chapter deals with planning where to go on snowshoes or skis, finding your way without many of the usual indicators, and dealing with route-finding problems peculiar to snow-covered landscapes.

Throughout the book I have illustrated the instruction with examples from the way-finding adventures of myself and my friends.

Make Things Easy on Yourself

You'll find the information in this book much easier to absorb if you read it with a compass and a topographic map at hand. You should borrow these tools from a fellow outdoor person if you aren't ready to buy your own. The discussion of maps will be even clearer if you can refer to the topographic map of an area you are already familiar with, but for starters any topographic map will do. If you want to get a compass now, skip ahead to page 47 for tips on a good hiker's compass.

2

The Tools of Wilderness Travel

Several tools can help you get around happily in the outback; they're what this book is all about. Some, such as technical aids, will be covered briefly now. Others need longer treatment and so warrant an entire chapter.

Without doubt, the single most important item in the toolbox is **you.** A clear, cool head atop a body in good condition, a lively curiosity and adventurous spirit tempered by good common sense—these are indispensable marks of a successful wilderness traveler. The sharpest map and compass user in the woods can still get into big trouble. His technical skills must be used within a framework of active good judgment which continuously sizes up other factors affecting his travels: weather, the physical and mental shape of each group member, the group's pace, progress over the terrain, and other matters.

Two Toolbox Essentials Are: Map and Compass

Maps are the basis for planning trips and successfully pulling them off. Map-talk is so vivid that it can help you estimate the hiking time and difficulty of each leg of your journey, locate water sources and choose perfect campsites. In an emergency, a map can provide alternate routes to safety. Maps present so revealing a picture of the terrain that it's hard to understand why people ever travel without them. But they frequently do, especially when intending to stay on a popular trail.

A **compass** is a simple device that gives a constant directional reference. Used by itself, without a map, a compass can:

■ measure the direction to something you can see and keep you headed on a straight line toward it.

■ help you get around a big obstacle on your travel line—such as a hill you'd rather go around than over—and pick up your line on the other side of it.

■ keep you moving straight toward some known base line such as a road.

- help you keep track of changes you make in direction.

- guide you to an unseen destination in a given direction, for example, a lake a friend has told you about.

- help you relocate some special place.

- tell you where the sun will rise or set.

- give you a rough estimate of the time of day.

When teamed with a map, a compass will:

- pinpoint your location.

- help you identify what you're looking at.

- keep you from missing a small destination such as your camp or car.

- let you measure, then follow, the direction from one place to another on the map, even if you can't see the goal because of distance or poor visibility.

Another part of the toolbox contains **natural route-finding aids,** things that were around long before we hit the trail: the sun, stars and vegetation. Paying more than casual attention to them can reward you with information about direction and a rough estimate of time, both of which influence your travels.

Extremely helpful **verbal and written information** can be gleaned from diverse sources: the local ranger, friends who've hiked the territory, townsfolk near the trailhead, weather reports, hiking guidebooks, outdoor magazines, trail descriptions. How to get and use these will be covered in "Route Planning."

Some **technical aids** that many outdoor trekkers swear by and others do very well without are binoculars, altimeter and map measurer. Standard binoculars are a bit too heavy and bulky for most backpackers, so all but the most dedicated animal and bird watchers usually leave them home. For route-finding, though, *some* kind of vision-extender is beneficial, and you might want to consider an alternative. If you have something that weighs a few ounces and fits in a pocket, you'll use it often. Most outdoor stores carry lightweight, compact **monoculars** ($30 and up) and **binoculars** ($130 and up). If you spend much time outdoors, the pleasure and aid one of these options can give are worth many times the price. They help you roam the wilds by:

- making identification of landmarks easier and more accurate—not just peaks and ridges, but your speck of a camp too.

- giving you a clearer feel for the overall patterns of the landscape you're exploring.

- helping you scout a route visually to avoid dead-end canyons, difficult water crossings and the like.

■ showing you alternative routes the naked eye can't adequately assess. Canyon walls that appear uniformly steep and unhikeable, for instance, are frequently threaded top to bottom with animal trails that make for adventurous walking. But you need to know first if the whole wall is passable; getting stymied by an overhanging rim is discouraging after struggling upward for two hours. I celebrated my forty-second birthday climbing out of southeast Oregon's Blitzen Gorge by such a binocular-scouted route, and was greeted by a soaring golden eagle at the top! The binoculars paid for themselves in one day.

An **altimeter** can help you determine your location by adding an elevation reading to other things you know. It's a kind of barometer which measures atmospheric pressure. A bit of fiddling is necessary: set at a known elevation before starting, check and reset at known points along the way. Because an altimeter is affected by weather changes, an approaching storm can produce a false reading. Altimeters are probably most useful to climbers and other habitual roamers of the high and often trailless reaches.

A **map measurer** (under $10) is helpful in trip planning. Set this little gadget down on the map and roll it along your proposed route for a readout on the distance. Realize, though, that to a backcountry walker "a mile" doesn't mean much without other information. In "Route Planning" we'll talk about this and other ways to assess distance on a map.

3

Maps

Without ever having been to a particular place, and without talking to someone who has, you can already know quite a lot about it.

> The trail begins at the end of a dirt road midway on the north side of a small clearing at 5600 feet elevation. For the first half-mile we'll climb gradually through trees, curving northeast around a small rise. Off the trail to the right we'll see scattered small meadows with some swampy areas—and possibly beavers? We'd better carry enough water to get us to camp, because the stream we cross at a half-mile might be dry. The climbing gets harder as the trail switchbacks up the south ridge of Songdog Mountain, and the view should be terrific when we break out of the trees at 6800 feet. We'll probably see all the way to Old Whiteface if the weather's good! And we'll be looking down on the Echo Lakes Basin.

The source of all these details is, of course, a map. A map gives a flat, symbolic, bird's-eye view of the earth's surface. Different kinds of maps present different kinds of information, and a hiker may need more than one. This section will tell you how to choose, get and use the maps you need.

Types of Maps

Highway maps and many maps published by state and federal land management agencies are **planimetric,** treating the ground as flat. They usually cover quite a large area, accurately place roads and towns, and give *rough* locations of peaks and large water features. Planimetric maps don't show valleys and hills. In planning a hike, you may need to know where current logging roads are, and their designations, which can change. A planimetric map will often be the best source of current information about these and other man-made features.

Pictorial relief maps give the illusion of showing the shape of the land—its hills, valleys and such. They can be helpful as aids in trip planning, but aren't sufficient for navigation.

A hiker's best friend is the **topographic** map. By the use of contour lines it gives a detailed picture of the shape of the land—the hills, depressions, flat places, cliffs and other features you'll need to know about if you explore that land on foot. Colors and symbols on this map indicate whether those hills are wooded or open, where you'll find water, where roads, power lines, trails and shelters are located, and many other valuable bits of information. Besides helping you get around in the outback, they're fun to use. From a high spot a map will show you where you've been and where you're going and help you identify peaks.

Topographic maps are developed by several agencies, but the basic and, generally speaking, most accurate ones come from the United States Geological Survey. For a given area the Forest Service or National Park Service may publish a recreational map based on USGS topographic data but with updated information on roads, trails, wilderness boundaries and such. USGS maps for many areas are more than twenty years old. If the one for your hiking territory hasn't been revised in the last few years, you should supplement or replace it with a recent topographic map from the Forest Service or another agency that oversees the area. The basic shape of the land is usually a long time in changing, but man's "improvements" have speedy consequences.

Most hikers' collections eventually contain several USGS "topos" (also called quadrangles or "quads"), some Forest Service topographic maps of federally designated wilderness areas, National Park Service

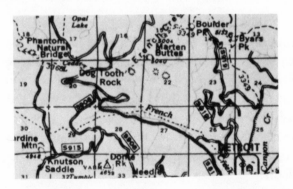

Planimetric Map, *1976, Forest Service* ▪ *No contour lines to indicate shape of the land* ▪ *No shading to show where land is forested or where open* ▪ *What is Rocky Top Trail on the topo is now a road* ▪ *Shows many more roads than the topographic* ▪ *Shows a trail along the north side of French Creek*

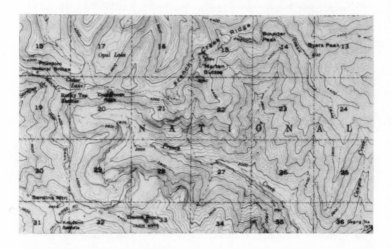

Topographic Map, 1956, USGS ▪ Contour lines show that the area is full of steep hillsides, with a few flat spots such as the large "table" north of Dome Rock ▪ Shading shows solid woods except for the beginnings of French Creek, the "table" and a few other spots ▪ Indicates a shelter at Rocky Top which probably is no longer there, since the trail passing it is now a road

topographic maps and planimetric Bureau of Land Management or national forest maps. A wide range of maps will provide a fuller picture of the place you want to visit, and will also help you avoid errors that cost energy and time.

(In all illustrations from topographic maps, we have used a gray screen to indicate what on your map is green shading.)

Whichever map you decide to use, be sure it is the *most recent revision*. Rather than assuming a two-year-old map is the newest one, check with authorities. Due to overuse and overcrowding, trails in popular areas are frequently rerouted.

Deciphering a Map

The aim in reading a topographic map is to picture the landforms and features that go with different patterns of contour lines, colors and symbols. Map-reading mastery will turn the language of squiggly lines, strange marks and irregular color patterns into a vivid mental image. After a bit of practice in the wild, you'll look at a map and see cliffs, meadows, irregular hills, a notched ridge, a sure water source, a pass that promises a great view. A feel for the shape of the area as a whole will emerge from your "reading" of the parts.

Speaking Topographically

A topographic map's key feature is its **contour lines,** whose patterns make little sense to the untrained eye. Each is an imaginary line on the ground at a constant elevation above sea level. If you trace with your finger a line labeled "6500," everywhere it goes on your map —around a ridge, into a gully, across a glacier—will be at 6500 feet above sea level. If you could walk that imaginary line on the ground, you'd be walking at a constant elevation, neither climbing nor dropping.

The empty space on the map between two contour lines represents an elevation change and is called the **contour interval.** The size of this interval stays constant on any one map, but varies from map to map depending on map scale and type of terrain. In flattish country the interval might be twenty feet, but in a mountainous area there wouldn't be room on the map for all the lines if such a small interval were used. More likely the interval would be forty, fifty or even eighty feet. (On some maps, broken supplementary contour lines divide the intervals even further.)

The interval will be printed at the bottom of your USGS map, or on the legend of other maps, as: CONTOUR INTERVAL 40 FEET. This means that each line is forty feet above or below the one next to it. Where the lines are jammed close together the land is very steep; you would cover the elevation gain or loss in a short horizontal distance. Where the lines are far apart you'd walk a longer distance to make the same gain or loss in elevation; the land would be gentler, sometimes nearly flat.

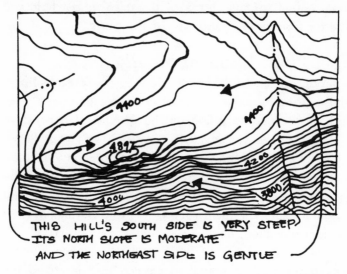

THIS HILL'S SOUTH SIDE IS VERY STEEP.
ITS NORTH SLOPE IS MODERATE
AND THE NORTHEAST SIDE IS GENTLE

Every fifth contour line, called an **index contour**, is darker; its elevation is printed in several places along it. Between pairs of darker lines are four lighter lines. On a map whose contour interval is forty feet, there are two hundred feet between index lines, forty feet between adjacent contour lines.

By reading the elevations printed along the index contours your trail crosses, you can figure out whether you'll be chugging uphill or sauntering downhill. And by noting how close together the contour lines are, you can gauge the steepness of the slope, as well as the energy and time needed to cover it. An elevation change of 1000 feet in a mile is considered respectably steep.

Keep in mind the contour interval for the map you're using, since a pattern of lines *by itself* doesn't mean much. Four bunched-up lines on a map with a twenty-foot interval represents only a sixty-foot rise, but the same four-line jam on a map with an eighty-foot interval shows a formidable 240-foot cliff!

Checking the contour interval also alerts you that there could be some features the map won't show. What looks gentle could be a series of ledges and slopes. A sixty-foot rise or dropoff won't be apparent on a map whose interval is eighty feet. I remember skiing pack-laden through an area that looked invitingly flat on the map but was in reality covered with irregular bumps just under the size of the contour interval, and took twice as long to negotiate as I had planned.

Patterns of contour lines are shorthand for some typical landforms. Study these configurations to fix them in your mind; pick them out on several maps; compare gullies and different mountain shapes with their map pictures each time you hike. Soon you'll be translating with ease.

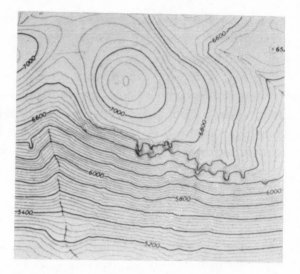

A series of concentric rings of contour lines shows a **hill or peak,** the top of which is in the inmost loop ▪ A flat-topped mesa will have an inner circle almost as large as the ones describing its side slopes ▪ The summit of a jagged peak will be in a tiny ring

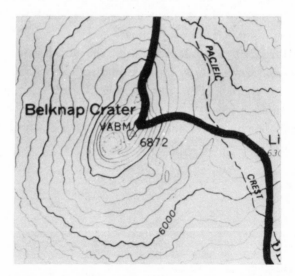

A closed circle or loop can also be a **depression,** indicated by tick marks inside the loop

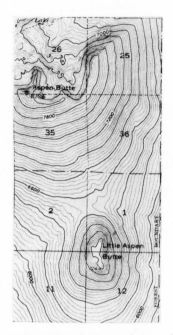

Two U-shaped sets of lines meeting bottom to bottom denote a **saddle or pass** between two higher areas

Lines very close together indicate a **steep wall or cliff**

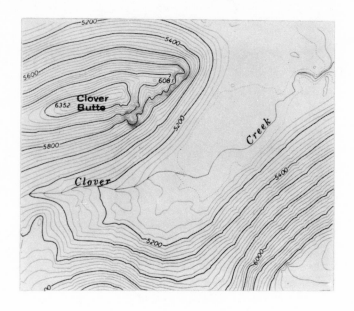

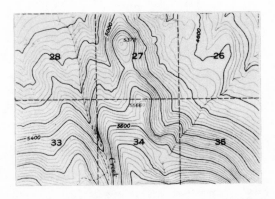

A **valley or gully** *is shown by a pattern of nesting U's or V's pointing upstream* ■ *Note dotted supplementary contour lines in Clover Creek's broad valley* ■ *In the other map, the creek on the left is in a steep gully; the one on the right barely dents the hill*

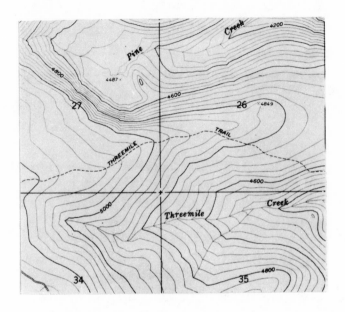

A **ridge** appears as a downhill-pointing U or V, depending on the sharpness of the crest ■ Threemile Trail follows the ridge between Pine Creek and Threemile Creek

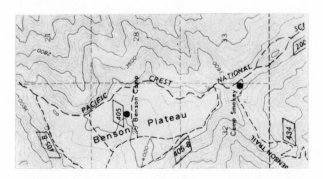

A **bench or flat shelf** in otherwise steeper terrain is pictured by parallel lines that suddenly spread apart ■ Benson Plateau is a flat shelf atop a steep-sided hill

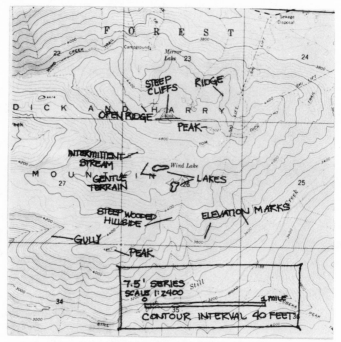

Five **colors** used on USGS maps add to the picture of the land (please refer to actual map, as the map above does not show colors).

> **green** Solid overprint for tree cover, irregular dots for scrub.
>
> **white** Untreed. Surface can be grassy or barren, with sand, small rocks, large boulders.
>
> **black** Man-made features such as campgrounds, roads, buildings, power lines, trails, shelters; county, state,

national forest boundaries; names; some elevations.

blue   Water features and names, including oceans, lakes, glaciers, swamps, springs. *Perennial* lakes and streams, which contain water all year, have solid lines; *intermittent* ones, seasonal, are shown by broken lines.

brown   Contour lines, their elevations, some peak elevations.

red   Some roads, urban areas, and U.S. land survey lines.

Photorevised maps will show changes with a purple overprint, but these revisions usually cover urban areas and a hiker isn't likely to find purple markings on his map.

Symbols can either be pictographs which resemble the objects they stand for or abstractions, and in both cases they are printed in colors consistent with their meaning. The tadpolelike sign for a spring will be blue, as will the bunches of vegetation indicating a swamp or marsh. Two colors in conjunction describe the feature and its setting. For instance, a marsh in a clearing is pictured by the blue marsh symbol on a white background; if the marsh is wooded, the blue symbol is on a green background; if the marsh is submerged, both symbol and background are blue.

COMMON MAP SYMBOLS

Paved road	▬▬▬▬▬▬▬
Light-duty road	═══════
Unimproved road	= = = = = ==
Railroad	—+—+—+—+—
Power line with located metal tower	·•----•----□----•---··
Buildings	▪ ∎ ◂
Trail	- - - - - - - - -
County boundary line	— — — — — -
Township or range line (red)	——————
Section line (red)	————————
Elevation marks	✕ 5466 △ 3112 BM ✕ 7018
Index contour	⌒ 5200 ⌒
Intermediate contour	⌒⌒

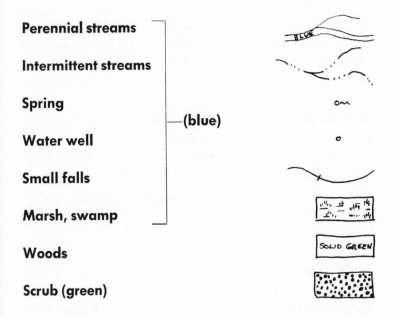

Perennial streams

Intermittent streams

Spring

Water well ⎤—(blue)

Small falls

Marsh, swamp

Woods

Scrub (green)

Elevations are noted in ways which indicate how the figure was obtained. While interesting, the distinctions are not usually vital. What *is* important is that marked elevations can help a foot traveler confirm or figure out his location.

High spots on the map may be marked with the elevation and an X, BM or VABM, and sometimes a triangle with a dot in it. These symbols are called **bench marks.** If you climb to the bench mark site, you'll probably find a permanent metal marker with the elevation printed on it. If this marker is in a brushy spot there might be a tree blaze or a paint spot on nearby rocks to help locate it.

Map elevations printed in black are considered more precise than those in brown. Some elevations were actually verified on foot; others were calculated from aerial photos or visual sightings from other points of known elevation. Don't confuse the X of an elevation mark with the larger "plus" signs showing where latitude and longitude lines would intersect if they were drawn in on the map.

COVERAGE AND SCALE. USGS topographic maps are bounded by parallels of latitude (east-west) and meridians of longitude (north-south), oriented to the geographic north pole, the upper end of the earth's axis. Latitude and longitude of the area enclosed by a map are printed at each corner in degrees ($^\circ$), minutes (') and seconds ("). Sixty minutes equals one degree.

Maps are published in several scales (also called "series"), but two are most useful to foot travelers. The 7.5-minute maps cover 7½ minutes of latitude and longitude, an area of about six by nine miles. A 15-minute map covers one quarter of a degree of latitude and longitude, or roughly twelve by eighteen miles. (Coverage depends on latitude; the closer an area is to the equator, the more square miles its map will cover.)

A 7.5-minute map covers one fourth the area of a 15-minute map and is printed on a slightly larger sheet of paper; it is easier to read and offers more detail. But it has a drawback: if a person needs to identify a landmark more than a few miles away, it will likely be off his map. Consequently, these maps don't give a broad picture of the land. Yet carrying all the adjacent maps can be cumbersome.

One solution is to use both the 7.5-minute map for your main area of travel and the 15-minute or Forest Service topographic for the bigger picture. Another is to get a 1:250,000 USGS map (published for most areas). An inch on a map of this scale equals about four miles,

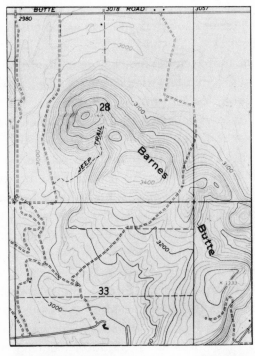

CAPTION 1

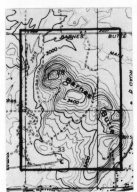

CAPTION 2

CAPTION 3

1. 7.5′-map (contour interval 20 feet) shows greatest detail
2. 15′-map (contour interval 40 feet) has less detail, but enough for foot travel
3. 1:250,000 map (contour interval 200 feet) covers larger area, shows only boldest detail

so the map will cover enough territory to encompass most landmarks you'll see.

A 15-minute map includes many more landmarks, and although there's a bit less detail shown, the scale is certainly adequate for foot travel.

There isn't always a choice of scale, but when areas are mapped in both you'll have to decide which suits your needs. On a trip of more than a day or two, you'd probably walk across a whole 7.5-minute quad; a week-long ramble could cover several. A backpacker traveling the length of Oregon on the 420-mile Skyline Trail migrates across twenty-five maps—sixteen 15-minute and nine 7.5-minute—in about a month.

The **scale** of a map is noted in the legend (lower margin of a USGS quad) and describes the relationship between distance on the ground and on the map. Scale is usually stated as a ratio or fraction. A 15-minute map has a scale of 1:62,500 (or 1/62,500), meaning one inch on the map equals 62,500 inches on the ground. Roughly translated, this means one inch covers about one mile. Very handy! On 7.5-minute maps the scale is 1:24,000 and a mile of ground is pictured by about 2½ inches of map. The smaller the denominator of the fraction, the more room for detail on the map.

Bar scales printed with a map's legend give a means of measuring distance on the map.

MORE MAP FEATURES. A map is **named** for some prominent feature in its bounds, with name and series printed at both the top and bottom of the sheet. On all four corners and sides you'll find the names of adjoining maps in parentheses, so you'll know which maps to get if your route goes beyond one map.

The **date** a map was originally issued is found under its name at the bottom, but even more important is the date of the most recent field-check, found at the lower left. Information on the map was accurate as of that year, but many changes could have since occurred. If the map is outdated, you may hike across unforeseen roads and power lines, or search in vain for a trail long since abandoned and overgrown or for a spring gone dry. Meadows and clear-cuts fill in with trees, avalanches smash through timbered mountainsides, swamps become ponds, shelters are built or torn down. Make sure you have the latest word, whether by talking with someone familiar with the area or by checking a more recent map put out by the agency that oversees the land (Bureau of Land Management, Forest Service, state agencies).

Another vital piece of information is found in the map's bottom margin: the angle diagram showing the area's **magnetic declination.** You must know this in order to use map and compass *together.* Of course, a map can be used alone with reasonable accuracy, but only when visibility is good. For further explanation of declination, see Chapter 5, "Putting Map and Compass Together."

As noted above, boundaries of counties, states, national forest and national park lands are usually printed in black with names on either side of the lines. Trails are also shown in black—by dotted lines—so make sure you don't plan to hike a county line.

Red vertical and horizontal lines frequently divide most or all of a map (USGS and topographic maps issued by other agencies as well) into squares with red numbers in the centers. These **U.S. Land Survey lines** assist hikers in both route planning and staying found.

The lines were developed to divide land into units one mile square called *sections*. Thirty-six sections are grouped into a larger square called a *township*, and the sections are numbered in a back-and-forth pattern always beginning at the top right corner.

SECTION 18

(ONE MILE SQUARE)

6	5	4	3	2	1
7	8	9	10	11	12
18	17	16	15	14	13
19	20	21	22	23	24
30	29	28	27	26	25
31	32	33	34	35	36

A TOWNSHIP

Townships are stacked in rows set off by vertical lines called *range lines* and horizontal lines called *township lines*. Small red letters and numbers along all four sides of the map refer to range and township designations.

Because each section is a mile square, it provides a quick estimate of distance on a map. And when you and a friend discuss an upcoming trip, you can use section numbers for ready reference: "How about exploring the long canyon in section 31?"

Land survey divisions sometimes help you confirm your

location, even get you unlost! There is frequently a **marker** set where section lines intersect; you can read the location from the marker and pinpoint it on your map. At some section corners the marker is a yellow metal plate printed with the numbered sections, also noting range and township numbers. A nail through the plate marks where you are.

The type of section corner marker used depends on when the land was surveyed and how much disturbance there has been since by fire, avalanche, acts of man or other derangements. It's still possible to find markers from surveys done in the 1800's, when a corner might have been designated by notches chipped into a large native stone, a blaze or sign on a "bearing tree" or a notched post.

Not all lands have been surveyed, so if you're exploring a wilderness area or national park you might never encounter public land system markers. In such places, elevation bench marks may be the only permanent evidence of survey work. (Occasionally a hiker comes on a post or stone marked during a mineral survey—MS followed by a number—but these aren't on the map.)

BUT THERE ARE LIMITS! A topographic map can tell you much about the land, but not everything. Some limitations have already been mentioned: not showing terrain features if their elevation difference is less than the contour interval; not registering recent changes in trails, roads, vegetation or land shape.

Another hitch is that you can't always judge how difficult a piece of terrain is by reading contour lines and colors. What the map indicates is a barren, formidably steep draw could be a negotiable scree slope offering relatively stable footing.

On a topographic map, white means simply that the area is free of trees and scrub, not what it *is* covered with—information that affects your travel even if there's a trail. You could be in for a trudge across sand, gravelly rocks, plate-sized slate slabs, big boulders to hop or weave through, grassy clumps on little hillocks, smooth flat "lawn" or endless variations on the treeless theme.

There are a couple of situations in which a map alone cannot get you where you want to go or keep you found. The obvious one is when thick woods or darkening weather limit visibility. Certain types of country are hard to figure out without the added help of a direction-finder. Both monotonous hill country and areas filled with lakes have so many similar features that you can't tell one hill or lake from another just by studying the map. (Enter the compass!)

Sources of Maps

USGS maps are sold in many outdoor stores (some also stock national forest and wilderness maps), some bookstores and other retail outlets (look in the Yellow Pages under "Maps"). Further, the USGS has ten Public Inquiries Offices which sell topographic maps over-the-counter and offer related services.

You can also order maps by mail from the addresses which follow. To figure out which map you need, request a free index for the state you want to hike in. This lists all available maps on a chart printed over the state's outline, as well as special maps—of national parks, for example—published for the area, addresses of local map dealers, map reference libraries and federal map distribution centers.

For areas east of the Mississippi River, including Minnesota, Puerto Rico and the Virgin Islands, write to:

Branch of Distribution
U.S. Geological Survey
1200 South Eads Street
Arlington, VA 22202

Indexes for areas west of the Mississippi River, including Alaska, Hawaii, Louisiana, Guam and American Samoa, are available from:

Branch of Distribution
U.S. Geological Survey
Box 25286, Federal Center
Denver, CO 80225

Alaska residents may get indexes directly from:

> **Distribution Section**
> **U.S. Geological Survey**
> **Federal Building, Box 12**
> **101 12th Avenue**
> **Fairbanks, AK   99701**

When you request an index, also ask for a free symbol sheet and folder describing topographic maps.

Order the map you want by name, series and state, and enclose a check or money order made out to the U.S. Geological Survey. The 7.5-minute and 15-minute maps are a bargain at $1.25 each; prices of other maps are listed on the index.

OTHER MAPS. In addition to the USGS topographic map, you may want to get a more recent map put out by the agency managing your hiking area. In most of the United States the wild places sought by foot travelers are controlled by one of four federal agencies: the Forest Service, the National Park Service, the Fish and Wildlife Service, or the Bureau of Land Management. A few states have more hikeable country that is state-owned: New York, Maine, Michigan, Wisconsin, Alaska, California.

The Forest Service has planimetric maps of its national forests, national grasslands and some national parks, and topographic maps of the wilderness areas within its territory. Some are free; others cost 50 cents or so. There are nine regional offices and, within each region, maps are also available at forest supervisors' offices and district ranger stations. The addresses of these places are listed in your phone book under "United States Government, Department of Agriculture."

The Bureau of Land Management has nine regional offices and oversees mainly desert terrain in the West and Southwest. The Fish and Wildlife Service, with six regional offices, is in charge of wildlife refuges. These two agencies, along with the National Park Service (eight regional offices), are listed under "United States Government, Department of Interior."

The USGS has a very helpful central information source that gives prompt, clear answers to any map-related questions you might want to ask:

National Cartographic Information Center
507 National Center
Reston, VA   22092

CANADIAN MAPS. Three free indexes list what's available from National Topographic System Maps of Canada. Order the index and whatever maps you want from:

Canada Map Office
615 Booth Street
Ottawa, Ontario
Canada   K1A OE9

This office will also send a provincial listing of topographic map dealers and a list of dealers outside Canada from whom individual maps may be bought.

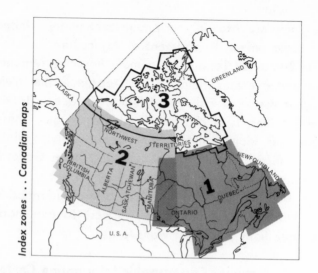

Index zones . . . Canadian maps

Use and Care of Maps

Maps are cheap and easily replaceable from your home base, but not in the outback, so take care to keep them in usable shape. A soggy map is soon unreadable.

Many travelers fold the portion in use outward and carry the map in a large plastic bag (heavier and more durable map cases are sold at outdoor stores). You can then consult the map without exposing it to the elements.

For a map you use often, a more permanent, slightly heavier alternative is to cover one or both sides with clear adhesive plastic (sold in houseware departments by the roll, along with the printed stuff used to cover shelves). This method does a better job of preserving what's on the folds and makes your map absolutely waterproof, and is especially good for rainy or snowy treks.

Maps can also be cut into sections and backed with dry mounting cloth (available at engineering supply outlets) in a somewhat more tedious process that produces a durable sheet.

If your route covers two adjoining maps, you can trim margins where they meet and tape the maps together from the back. A caution: save any marginal information you might need, especially from the bottom legend, and transfer important data to the backs of the maps.

Occasionally your hike might cover territory at the corners of two to four maps. Cut and join these sections into one map that gives you a readier glimpse of the whole area, being careful to match contour lines at the edges and to write on the back of each piece the name of the original map.

If your trip is long, your pack crammed full and your mind bulk-conscious, it's easy to get carried away with trimming and leaving adjacent maps home. *Don't overdo it!* To save bulk and weight on a long ski trip through Crater Lake National Park, we lifted from the center of the map just the small part our route covered. When we tried to identify landmarks a few miles away, we bemoaned our economy.

What Can You Do with a Map?

The best way to learn map-reading is to leisurely spend time in an area you know well. In the same way you might take a hike specifically to watch birds or to learn to identify mushrooms, take one to study maps.

Compare what you see with its picture on the map. Start with the most prominent features: peaks, large clearings, lakes, drainages. Then carefully decipher the less obvious: smaller hills, ridges, streams. You won't get it all down firmly on one hike, but every bit of practice will help you visualize from the map symbols and develop a sense of scale about distances and elevations.

MATCHING MAP AND LANDSCAPE. As long as visibility is good and you can identify a couple of landmarks, you can line up your map without a compass. This is called "orienting by visual inspection" and is done by sighting across landmarks on the map to their counterparts in the terrain.

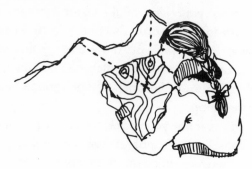

WHAT AM I LOOKING AT? If you know where you are and can orient the map as above, you can identify unknown landmarks around you. Line up your map, then put one end of a straightedge—a stick, pencil, edge of a notebook—on your map location and pivot it to point at the actual feature you want to identify. Study this line of sight on the map to see what features lie along it. Compare their shapes, tree patterns, elevations and rough distances from you with the unknown feature.

WHICH IS MOUNT MAGNIFICENT? You know where you are and perusing the map tells you that Mount Magnificent should be in view from here. You can see several peaks that might be it. To find out which one it is, orient your map, then lay a straightedge on the map so that it touches both your location and Mount Magnificent. Sighting along the straightedge and across the terrain, you'll see that mountain and maybe some others. Closely relate their shapes, relative elevations and distances from you with the map to decide which one is Mount M.

WHERE AM I? One very helpful bit of map work is discovering your location by sighting on known landmarks, which is called "triangulation." Later we'll see how to do this more precisely with the aid of a compass, but in good visibility the same basic procedure done with map alone can give you a rough estimate of where you are.

If you know you are somewhere on a given line such as a trail, stream or ridge, then you can plot your approximate location by sighting on just one known landmark. Orient your map by lining it up with known terrain features, and be careful not to move the map while you make your sightings. Put one end of a straight stick on the symbol of an identifiable landmark and point the other end at the actual landmark. Extend the line made by this pointer by putting a second straight stick on the map along the line of sight. Where this line crosses your trail, stream or ridge is where you are. If you can make a second sighting on another known landmark—preferably around 90 degrees, or a quarter-circle, away from the first—you'll have an even more accurate "fix."

What **if you have no idea where you are but can see and identify two landmarks?** Simply take sightings with straight sticks, as above, and plot the lines of sight on your map. Where the lines intersect is your approximate location. And again, three sightings can pinpoint it even better.

Remember that there are some situations in which a map alone isn't sufficient to guide your travels or keep

you from getting lost: in limited visibility and in certain kinds of terrain. Then you need the added help of a direction-finder.

The next two chapters describe, respectively, several basic procedures with a compass alone and methods which use map and compass together.

4

Compass

This simple palm-sized gadget, with so few parts that you can count them on your fingers, has bailed out many a bewildered hiker.

> Compass in his pocket, a Scout leader left base camp to go out for supplies. Because the trail was "clear" he took no map. On his return trip the trail became vague where it reentered the woods after crossing a meadow. My friend veered slightly in the wrong direction. Slightly is all it takes; after a half-mile, nothing looked familiar. Resisting that sinking feeling, he climbed a high spot and cased the terrain until he recognized a rockpile he had noticed near camp. A compass bearing to the rockpile gave him a straight line to travel. Home again, with the goods!

This comforting device also makes possible wanderings that otherwise would be foolhardy.

> For two days a steady snowfall hid from view all the spectacular scenery we knew was there: frozen lakes, big and little hills,

one *stunning peak. Sure, it was disappointing not to be able to see anything beyond a quarter-mile or so, but we had a grand time anyway, skiing up and down and all over an area about four miles square. Until the afternoon we headed home, we never knew our exact location. Were we worried? No, because our prior knowledge of the country, combined with a compass, kept us unlost: we used a base line. A conveniently placed highway ran east-west, and we were skiing north of it. So wherever we were, heading south would take us to this road. Sure enough, we eventually topped out on a rise and spotted an identifiable lake, a bit north of the highway and two miles east of the car.*

Those of us who stray off streets and highways need an artificial direction-finder simply because we aren't naturally equipped with one. We can rely to some extent on natural aids like the sun, and on landmarks when we can see and recognize them. But with a compass our ranging isn't restricted to familiar territory or to clear days; we can change from passive tourist to active explorer.

A compass is basically a magnet mounted on a pivot, free to turn in response to the pull of the earth's magnetic field. The housing protects the needle and helps you relate the direction in which the needle points to directions on the map and on the land. A compass by itself can't tell you where you are, but it *can* tell you about direction—which is a lot more than your instincts can do!

What Makes a Good Hiker's Compass?

There are dozens of styles and models of compasses, designed for different uses. A hiker doesn't need to pay for or cart around the elaborate, precise, costlier, heavier compass a surveyor needs.

The orienteering compass designed in Sweden in the 1930's has several features helpful to a wilderness route-finder. It's the type of compass most often sold in outdoor stores (Silva and Suunto are the main manufacturers) and most often carried by hikers. Its unique design makes compass operations so simple that hardly anyone fiddles with the old round pocket compass anymore. The price is reasonable ($5 and up) and the product durable and functional. Helpful features include:

■ a rotating housing with both cardinal points (N, E, S, W) and degrees (0–360) marked clockwise on the rim, with intermediate degree marks every five degrees or, better, every two degrees.

- a liquid-dampened needle whose north-seeking end is colored or marked in some other clear way.

- a transparent base plate on which the housing is mounted. It has a direction-of-travel arrow for sighting and following bearings, and straight edges which make it easy to measure and plot directions on a map.

- an orienting arrow printed on the bottom of the housing.

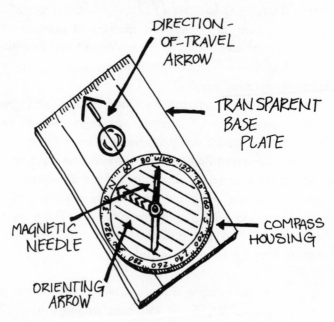

Deflection

Because a compass needle aligns itself with the earth's magnetic field, it can be confused by nearby metallic or magnetic objects. Occasionally some local magnetic disturbance or large iron deposit will throw a compass off. The cause is usually man-made: knife, belt buckle, camera or light meter, eyeglass rims, wire fence, power line, steel eating utensils, zipper. If it's close enough to the compass needle, even an object as small as a paper clip can mess things up.

> *My snow-camping students stood patiently in a cold-footed cluster, mittened hands manipulating compasses as we practiced taking bearings to fix our location. Everyone reached close agreement except for one fellow, whose readings put us somewhere in the next county. Our search for a possible deflecting object finally unearthed the culprit: a can of foot powder buried in his front-riding beltpack!*

When you shop for a compass, make sure that there's no bubble in the housing, and that the needle swings freely and points in the same direction as the others in the store.

Compass Directions

Remember when you learned in high school geometry that a circle is divided into 360 degrees? Well, a compass face is simply a circle marked off in degrees by numbers from zero to 360. Measured clockwise from the top (zero degrees, or north), a fourth of the way around the circle is an angle of 90 degrees, or east. South, being exactly a half-circle across from north, is located at 180 degrees. A second set of markers divides the compass

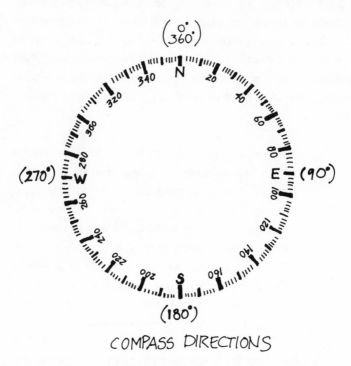

COMPASS DIRECTIONS

face into quarters: the cardinal points N, E, S, and W (north, east, south, west).

Using a Compass

SETTING A BEARING. To familiarize yourself with the basic uses of a compass, turn the movable housing until N lines up with the direction-of-travel arrow. (Some models are also labeled "Read bearing here.") You have *set a bearing* of north, which is the same as zero degrees or 360 degrees. After checking around for deflecting objects, hold the compass horizontal in front of you at an easy reading distance. Now turn your body and the compass as one until the north-seeking end of the needle lines up over the orienting arrow. You have *pointed yourself on a bearing* toward magnetic north. (Magnetic north is different from map north or true north, but don't worry about that now; I'll explain it later.) To

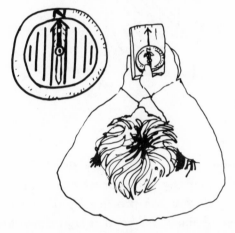

follow that bearing, you'd move along the line the direction-of-travel arrow points.

Now choose another bearing, or direction toward something, of 140 degrees. Turn the housing until 140 lines up with the direction-of-travel arrow. Turn body and compass until the north-seeking needle-end lines up over the orienting arrow. The direction-of-travel arrow tells you which way to go to follow a bearing of 140 degrees (as shown on the next page).

You can see that this system lets you pick any bearing, set it and get yourself pointed in that direction. There will be more later about how to travel that way.

MEASURING A BEARING. The next basic compass skill is to *measure the bearing (direction) to some landmark*

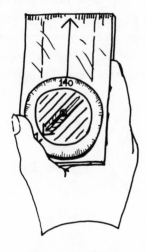

you're looking at. This is done by simply reversing the steps. First, point the direction-of-travel arrow at the landmark, which you can practice by aiming at a lamp in the corner of the room or at a sign down the street. Second, turn the housing until the orienting arrow lies under the north-seeking end of the needle. Third, read the bearing where the direction-of-travel line intersects the dial. Now you know the exact direction to the landmark you chose, expressed as an angle.

These two simple procedures—setting a bearing, measuring a bearing—are basic to getting around and knowing where you are in the wild.

FOLLOWING A BEARING. You've decided on a day hike to Basket Butte, whose bare top you can see about a mile from camp. You've measured the bearing to the butte. Now, how do you get there? If you could keep the goal in sight all the way, of course, you wouldn't need any other guide. But you know Basket Butte will disappear from view when you enter the trees ahead, and when the rolling terrain dips.

With a compass, you can travel a reasonably straight line to your destination even when you lose sight of it on the way. The trick is to pick **intermediate landmarks** along the line from you to the goal, traveling the distance in short legs from one landmark to another. To do this, follow these steps:

> **1.** Measure the bearing. Once this bearing is set, *don't* turn the housing at any time while you're following the bearing.

> **2.** Look ahead along the line of the direction-of-travel arrow and choose a landmark you can keep in sight and get to from your starting point—perhaps a distinctive boulder or snag on the far side of a huge clearing. In dense trees the best intermediate landmark might be only fifty feet away.

> **3.** Ignore the compass and walk to this landmark by the easiest route. Don't walk with head bent, peering at the compass and tripping over logs.

> **4.** When you get to the snag or rock you must make *sure* you are again headed in the right direction, on your original bearing line. To do this, hold the compass in front of you —don't touch that housing!—and turn body and compass until the north-seeking needle-end matches the orienting arrow.

WRONG
NO INTERMEDIATE LANDMARKS

RIGHT
USING INTERMEDIATE LANDMARKS

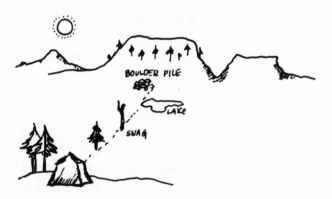

5. Pick another landmark along the bearing line and walk to it. Repeat this process as often as needed to cover the distance between camp and Basket Butte.

KEEPING ON YOUR BEARING BY BACKSIGHTING.

When traveling along a line of sight between landmarks you may occasionally lose the one you're headed for and wonder if you're still on the right line. To check, sight back to the landmark you started from. Face the starting landmark, compass in hand. Don't turn the housing! If you're on the right line, the "south" (or non-colored) end of the needle will line up over the orienting arrow. If it doesn't, move to one side or the other until it does.

"SOUTH" END OF NEEDLE!

BACK-BEARINGS. During lunch atop Basket Butte you had a great view for miles around, including the bright tent-specks of camp on the far side of that big clearing. Now, to get back. You know that once you're off the hill, camp will be hidden from view.

In essence, your course will be the reverse of the one that got you here, exactly opposite on the compass circle. If your original bearing was 60 degrees, the opposite number on the dial (a half-circle or 180 degrees away) would be 240 degrees (60 + 180 = 240). If the original bearing is more than 180 degrees, simply subtract the half-circle. A bearing of 300 degrees would have a back-bearing of 120 degrees (300 − 180 = 120).

That's the concept. There are two ways to follow a back-bearing, both easy.

■ In the first method you figure the new return bearing as above and reset it on the compass, then travel by intermediate landmarks as before.

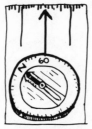 

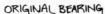

ORIGINAL BEARING   NEW BEARING

■ In the alternate method you don't change the compass at all. Instead, turn the whole compass around, keeping the original bearing set, so the direction-of-travel arrow points at your belly button and the *non-north* end of the needle lines up over the orienting arrow under the housing, just as it did in backsighting. Travel by orienting yourself with this different method of needle-matching and by sighting landmarks along the back end of the direction-of-travel arrow.

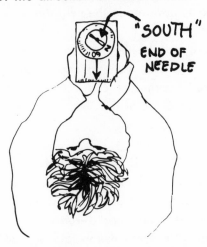

"SOUTH" END OF NEEDLE

I prefer the first method, setting a new bearing, since I like to have things clearly spelled out.

In the above example your starting and ending points were clear, but in any situation where they aren't so conspicuous you should leave a visible marker at both terminals of your route. Then, if you don't hit the exact spot after traveling the right time and distance, mark where you are and search in a widening spiral for your destination point.

KEEPING TRACK OF DIRECTION. A compass kept handy as you hike can be pulled out for frequent quick checks on the direction you're traveling. Suppose that map study at home and along the way indicated that your trail generally heads west for the first two miles. Are you moving in the direction you ought to be? Point the direction-of-travel arrow ahead along the trail, and turn the housing until the arrows line up. Read the bearing where the direction-of-travel arrow intersects the dial. Allowing for inevitable meanderings of the trail, is the bearing somewhere in the neighborhood of 270 degrees, or west?

There may be times when trail markings or signs are unclear and you want to ease your mind about where you are. A compass check on direction can either reassure you or point out that you're probably not where you want to be.

TRAVEL TOWARD A BASE LINE. This is one of the simplest applications of compass skills, but it could be the one that gets you unlost. A base line is a long, fairly straight linear landmark—roads and coastlines are the best, but often your hiking territory will include a ridge, a power-line cut, the shore of a long lake, or a generally straight river. What's important is that you know what direction the base line is from you, so you can hike toward it and ultimately figure out where *you are*. Don't worry about traveling a straight line; the general direction will get you to some point on that road or river.

All you need is a general knowledge of the area, which will enable you to choose a feature to use as a base line. If you have a map, the problem is solved. It's good to figure out the base-line possibilities *before* your hike. Then, even if you lose the map, you can get unlost as long as you have a compass that will guide you toward the base line.

Long straight roads are good base lines, even if

they're snow-covered. But you could unwittingly cross a trail if it had a snow cover or somehow wasn't clear. A friend and I know we crossed the Pacific Crest Trail on our ski outing north of the base-line road, because we started west of it and ended east, but we weren't aware of it when we crossed. That trail wouldn't have been a good winter base line. Big rivers make unmistakable base lines, but small streams can sometimes be mis-identified.

THE OLD 1–2–3. Here's a wilderness maneuver that makes use of three ideas we've covered:

> **1.** measuring the bearing to a landmark.

> **2.** using that bearing as a base line when you want to take a side excursion.

> **3.** getting home on the back-bearing of your original bearing.

From camp you sight on a notch in the ridge to the west, knowing you want to explore some small lakes that lie a bit north of that line. Think of the camp-to-notch bearing as a base-line "trail" by which you will return after your side trip to the lakes.

Head out on the original bearing (280 degrees in this example) and move north "off trail" when you know

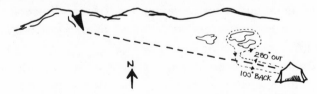

you're close to the lakes. When you're ready to go back to camp, walk south to your base-line "trail." How will you know when you reach this invisible trail? Take periodic bearings on the notch as you hike south. When the bearing reads 280 degrees, you're back on the original line. Now figure the back-bearing to camp (280 — 180 = 100) and travel it.

The key to this procedure is to be very careful about recording the *exact* point and view of the landmark you use for the original sight and to sight on that same spot later. A definite notch, for instance, is more precise than the top of a round hill.

With any route-finding procedure that's at all complex or involves more than one bearing which must be remembered, you should make notes about the important parts.

DELIBERATE ERROR. I'm not talking about getting lost on purpose, but about a special technique for avoiding that situation. When you're heading for a base line, sometimes it's because you want to get to a certain point on that line—maybe where your car is parked on a road.

Say you hike south after leaving the car on an east-west road. If you try to return to the car by the exact back-bearing, north, the chances are pretty good you'll miss it. That's not disastrous, since you'll at least be on the road somewhere. But which way should you turn to reach the car? You'll just have to guess, and possibly waste time and energy going the wrong direction. If you've come out to get help for an injured companion, that lost time could be crucial.

Deliberate error makes the right guess for you. Instead of following a back-bearing that you hope will lead to the point on the base line, you can deliberately plan to hit the line to one side or the other of your destination. Then, when you reach the base line you'll know which way to turn.

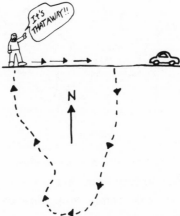

GETTING AROUND OBSTACLES. You're well on your way to Basket Butte. Coming over a small rise in the trees, you find a sizable lake smack on the line of travel. It's a clear day and you can see across this barrier, but you'll have to walk off-course to get around it.

There are two ways to handle this kind of situation and avoid the error that could creep in. The aim, of course, is to resume travel on the right line once you clear the obstacle. That seems obvious until you remember that just lining yourself up on the right bearing won't do it. For instance, along that lake shore there are an infinite number of 60-degree bearings which lie parallel to each other, but only one connects your starting point and destination!

The simplest solution is to sight a distinctive landmark on the opposite shore that is on your bearing line. Note carefully the point on the near shore where you head off

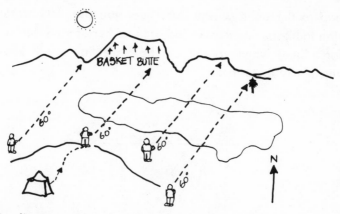

the line, marking it in some nondestructive, temporary way if you have to; it's a very common error to skip this step, and thus to lose your line. Then walk around to the opposite landmark. Things look different from a distance and from other angles, so to be certain the landmark is the one you sighted on, *backsight* to the point you left on the other shore. If the "south" end of the compass needle doesn't line up over the orienting arrow, move along the edge of the lake until it does.

In some situations there won't be a suitable landmark on the opposite shore. Find or make a landmark where you are, then move around the lake and backsight toward the marker you left until you're on the original bearing line again.

These two methods work fine if you can see around the obstacle in your path. But suppose the block is a huge, jumbled boulder pile you can't see over and certainly don't want to climb through? Or suppose a low fog hangs over the lake, obscuring the far shore? Or that clouds, rain or snow limit visibility in the whole area?

Then there's only one way to get around the obstacle

and have any hope of picking up your line on the other side. It involves pacing away from the course at a known angle—preferably a right angle.

Here's how. Faced with the obstacle, turn at a right angle and walk until you're past the swamp or rockpile, *counting your steps* as you go. Once past the end of it, resume your original bearing and move forward again until you've cleared the obstacle. Then make a right angle turn heading *back* to your original course and go *the same number of paces.*

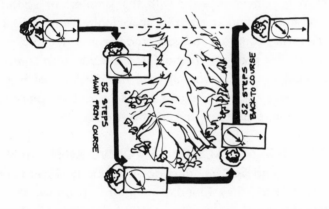

The orienteering compass base plate lets you make the right-angle turns without doing any calculations or resetting bearings; besides eliminating fuss, this rules out the possibility of mathematical errors and forgetting your original bearing. You simply sight across the *back edge* of the base plate during the two paced legs of the detour —while keeping the needle and orienting arrow lined up—and sight normally along the direction-of-travel arrow the rest of the time. The compass remains pointed the same way throughout this maneuver, but *you* move around it. During the paced stretches the compass will be held crosswise in your hand, pointing left when you turn right and right when you turn left.

Having a mind uneasy with the simplest of spatial relationships, I find it clearest to actually walk around the unmoving compass for each change in order to point myself in the proper direction. Maybe you won't need to do that. In the illustration, note the positions of hiker and compass for each leg of the detour. The compass doesn't change position, but the hiker does.

RELOCATING A PLACE ONCE YOU'VE BEEN THERE.
When Sam and Sal ventured down a barely discernible overgrown trail, they found a delightful meadow. They definitely wanted to be able to find this special place again, but since the takeoff point from the main trail was so unclear, they took steps to fix the junction's location in their memory. Physically marking the spot would undoubtedly lead others to their private discovery. Instead, Sam and Sal marked it in another way.

Back at the junction, they searched the surrounding terrain for a prominent landmark and took a bearing on it, then made a note: "Junction to our meadow: Go west on Tamarack Trail until the north end of the bald ridge is at 72 degrees." To make the hiking a bit easier, they might also have noted the bearing on which the overgrown trail starts off: "Trail starts through larches at 118 degrees."

I've used this technique frequently in areas that I first hike in summer and to which I want to return on skis in winter months. With several feet of snow cover, even major trails are often elusive. The only modification I make then in the basic procedure is to use a fairly close landmark for the crucial bearing, since poor winter visibility is likely to limit my viewing range.

This basic procedure of traveling on a known line until you reach a spot marked by one bearing is a variant on the base-line method and is useful in many different situations. You might want to hike along a ridge line until you reach a draw which leads to a good beaver pond at the base of the hill. But the ridge overlooks many draws, so you should "mark" the one you want with a bearing from that spot to some prominent feature.

On another hike you follow a stream about a mile and discover some interesting caves out of sight up the

east bank. Go back to where you left the stream and get a bearing on some landmark you'd be sure to see when you come back again, perhaps some lichen-covered crags upstream. On return trips to areas such as this, you travel the base-line stream until you reach the particular spot "marked" by the cross-bearing to the chosen landmark.

A step beyond this method for relocating a spot is when you must use *two* bearings: one for the first line of travel (the base line) and the second to find the spot on that line. You could use this method to find a cached food supply, the area of a big lake where the fishing was terrific or a can of water you stashed for a desert hike.

When you bury the water supply, mark it and take a bearing back to a landmark along the approach line of your future hike. Choose something prominent and permanent so you can count on finding it later. Write this bearing down: "Cache about ten minutes' walk from south end of layered cliff face, bearing 210 degrees." Now look for a second landmark, preferably close to 90 degrees away from the first; this will give you a more accurate "fix" than if you use landmarks too close together or too far apart. Twin buttes rise off to the east a bit, so you note: "Saddle between buttes, 138 degrees."

On the return trip, you reach the first landmark, the south end of the layered cliff face. To head on the line that will lead to your cache, check the bearing in your notes. Because you're now hiking the *back-bearing* of that, subtract 180 from the original 210, and head out on 30 degrees. When you've walked for almost ten minutes, begin taking bearings on the saddle between the twin buttes. When the bearing reads 138 degrees, you should be very near your cache.

Walking in the Real World

You'll note in the illustration above that the travel lines aren't straight. Our hiker isn't drunk or daydreaming. He just makes inevitable small detours in following his general bearing—around the end of a big log in the way, skirting a rise instead of going over the top, avoiding a squishy low spot.

Actual hiking can rarely be done in a straight line, since land has so many irregularities. The idea is to be conscious of the deviations you make off your course, keep them short, and try to zig as often as you zag. If you must make a sizable move, however, you're better off plotting a new bearing.

Given the necessity of occasional detours and the fact that a compass isn't perfectly precise, you'll be surprised at how close you can usually come to your destination. Moreover, you improve the odds when you:

- make careful, accurate sightings on both destination and intermediate landmarks.

- follow the direction-of-travel arrow, *not* the compass needle, when walking a bearing.

- recheck bearings carefully to avoid an accumulation of small errors.

- use bearings over *short* distances when possible.

- aim for a line rather than a point, when feasible; for instance, a stream is easier to hit than a waterfall on that stream.

- line up two distant objects on your bearing line that will always be in sight—for example, a prominent tree and a crag. When

you have to detour off course, you can correct for error by lining up these points.

■ continually relate your progress to the
map.

5

Putting Map and Compass Together

Using a map with a compass is easy when you hike near a line that runs through Twin City, Ontario; Rhinelander, Wisconsin; Kankakee, Illinois; Gadsden, Alabama; and Blountstown, Florida. Along that line a compass needle points toward the geographic north pole, **true north**, the direction most maps call north.

Elsewhere it's not quite as simple, and most North American hikers find that their compasses point either a bit east or west of true north. The needle doesn't really point *to* anything, but it tries to line up with the earth's magnetic field. Greatly simplifying, we say these irregular magnetic lines meet at the magnetic north and south poles, and that a compass needle points to one of the two slowly changing areas. The 1981 location of the north magnetic polar region is about 950 miles from the geographic north pole, in the Parry Islands of the Canadian Arctic.

Actually, in large areas of the world a compass needle may point ten degrees or more *away* from the direction of the magnetic pole. No matter. What's important to a foot traveler is a clear understanding that the compass needle doesn't point to true north.

The difference between true north and where your compass points is called **magnetic declination** or, sometimes, **variation.** This difference varies from place to place and changes very slowly from year to year. In order to use a map and compass together you need to know the declination for your hiking area. All good topographic maps will give this information for the year the map was issued. On USGS maps there's an angle diagram in the lower left margin showing the relative positions of true and magnetic north and the declination in degrees.

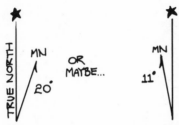

In North America this declination can be anything from zero to 35 degrees east (in Gordon, Alaska). Hikers near Caribou, Maine, have a westerly declination of about 21 degrees. As we noted, some lucky folks travel along a line where the declination is zero degrees. This is called the **agonic** line; the others are **isogonic** lines. Those of us with anything other than a zero-degree declination must make an adjustment when we use a map—which is laid out along *true* north-south lines—with a compass.

Lest you be tempted to ignore the declination and hope it won't matter, consider these consequences. For *each* degree ignored, you'll be off one sixtieth of whatever distance you travel. Translated, that's eighty-eight feet per degree in a mile of walking. Multiply that eighty-eight feet by your declination, and you could be lost! A hiker in northern Maine (declination 21 degrees west)

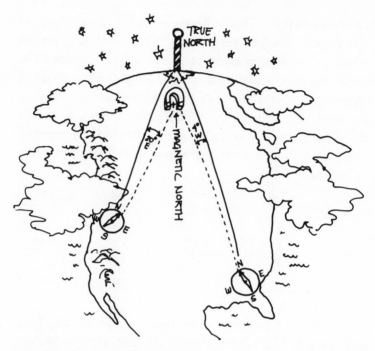

traveling to a lake a mile away would end up more than a third of a mile from his goal. In west Texas (declination 10 degrees east) the error would be one sixth of a mile in a mile of travel, still enough to confuse a person pretty thoroughly.

The earth's magnetic field is irregular, and the lines along which declination is the same are not neatly parallel. Hence declination sometimes changes abruptly and in strange patterns over the earth's surface. The 20 degrees east declination line, for example, flows like a huge winding river over the world, but the declination is the same at all points it touches.

Declination lines indicate only the approximate declination for any point they touch (actually an average for that area). The compass needle *doesn't* point in the direction of the lines.

Fortunately, declination is fairly constant in a given area from one mile to the next. Irregularities in the earth's magnetic field create spotty "declination anomalies," but odds are you could roam a lifetime and never encounter one. Daily and even seasonal variations in declinations are so small that a hiker's compass won't register the changes. Therefore, once you've determined the declination for the territory you're exploring, adjust for it and trust the compass over your instincts about direction.

One more caution. The declination printed on a map was accurate when the map was published, yet may be a bit unreliable if many years have elapsed. Declination changes slowly, and at unpredictably varying rates over the earth. In some places in certain years there's no annual change—as in 1980 along a line through southern Maine and parts of Quebec, and another through the Aleutian Islands toward Hawaii. Yet in other areas of North America the declination may increase or decrease as much as one sixth of a degree in a year. That may not sound like much, considering a compass isn't all that precise. But the USGS topographic map for an area may be thirty years old, and it's possible to have a change of five degrees in that period.

You can find out the current declinations for various areas and their rates of change by spending $3 on a fascinating chart available from the USGS: *Magnetic Declination in the United States—1980, Map I-1283.* This chart, updated every five years, can be ordered from the addresses on page 37. By referring to the chart you can update the declinations on your old maps, and

Magnetic declination in North America—1980. CREDIT: U.S. Geological Surve

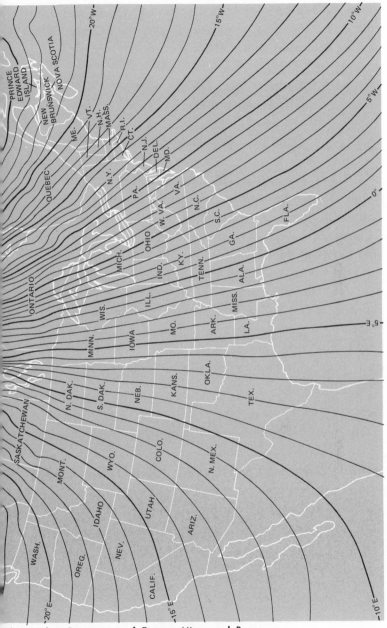

nd Canadian Department of Energy, Mines and Resources

the result will be a more accurate use of your map and compass. Canada's Magnetic Declination Chart 1980 ($2.50, including postage) may be purchased from:

> **Canada Map Office**
> **615 Booth Street**
> **Ottawa, Ontario**
> **Canada   K1A OE9**

When Does Declination Matter?

If you are using a compass alone as a constant direction-finder, in the ways described in the chapter called "Compass," you don't need to think about the relationship between your compass directions and true north.

When you use map and compass together, however, you need to adjust for the declination. (Another situation arises when you are using your compass to measure things in relation to the sun, which, like a map, works with reference to true north. "True Directions" and "Looking to Nature for Help" will guide you through these procedures.)

Adjusting for Declination

Always orient map and compass together as the first step in any procedure. Essentially, orienting the map with the compass adjusts for declination once and for all. You can make the correction accurately and then forget about it. And you can accomplish this matching of map and real world even if you don't know any landmarks or can't see through the fog beyond the tent door!

Here's what you do. Spread your map out on the levelest place you can find, lining it up approximately with the landscape if you can see. Check around for metal objects which could confuse the compass needle. Now turn the compass housing so that N is exactly at the top, lined up with the direction-of-travel arrow. With N toward the top of the map, place one side edge of the base plate along either of the side longitude lines of the map. (The red land survey lines aren't always true north-south.)

Holding the map and compass in this position, carefully turn them together until:

1. for an easterly declination: the north-seeking end of the needle points to the number on the dial which is your declination (find the declination number in the lower map margin).

2. for a westerly declination: the needle points to 360 minus the declination.

The map is now "oriented." Directions on the map match directions in the country around you. Anchor the edges of the map with rocks, sticks, or any non-metal gear. It's *very* important that the map remain oriented during all map and compass procedures. *Once the map is in this position, don't move it!*

Where Are We, Anyhow?

In the city, you can determine or describe your location by referring to the intersection of the street you're on and the nearest cross-street. In the wild, the same idea—

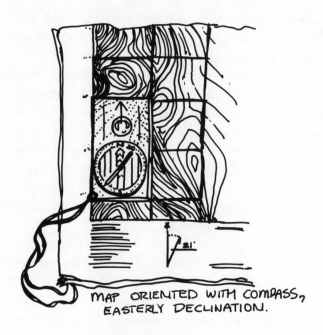

MAP ORIENTED WITH COMPASS,
EASTERLY DECLINATION.

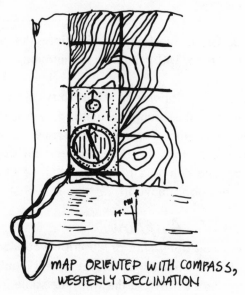

MAP ORIENTED WITH COMPASS,
WESTERLY DECLINATION

locating yourself by the intersection of lines—can show you approximately where you are.

If you know you are somewhere along a line—trail, ridge, stream—then you already know one line and need only one more in order to find your location on the map. If you aren't on a known line, you need at least *two* lines and, for a more precise fix, three.

To get the lines you need, take bearings on identifiable landmarks. When these bearings are plotted on the map their intersecting lines mark where you are. This procedure is called "triangulation," "resection," and "cross-bearings."

Here's how to do it. First, orient and anchor your map. Look around for a landmark some distance away that you can identify on the map and take a bearing on it: point the direction-of-travel arrow at a particular part of the landmark—not just a hill, but the highest part; not just a cliff face, but its north end. Turn the housing until the orienting arrow lies under the north-seeking end of the needle. The bearing from you to the landmark can be read where the direction-of-travel arrow intersects the dial, but you don't really need to know what it is in order to plot it on the map. Just don't turn the housing once the bearing is taken.

Now place the compass on the oriented map with one *front* base-plate corner right on the symbol for the landmark, being sure to use the part of the feature you took the bearing on. *Don't move the map!* Keeping this corner in place as a pivot, rotate the *whole* compass, base plate and all, until the orienting arrow and the needle are again lined up. You have recreated on the map the line you measured in the air.

Draw a line along the base-plate edge running

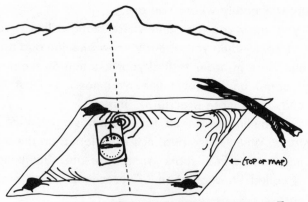

WHEN YOU WONDER WHERE YOU ARE,
PLOT A BEARING TO A KNOWN LANDMARK
... YOU'RE SOMEWHERE ON THAT LINE!!

through the landmark (mark the line with a pine needle if you don't have a pencil). If you already knew you were on a given line, this landmark bearing will cross the line at your approximate location.

If you had no idea about your position, the landmark bearing tells you that you are *somewhere* along the bearing line. To find out where, take a bearing on a second landmark and plot it on the map in the same way. You may need to extend the lines until they cross, but at their intersection is your location. If they don't cross, you probably plotted one or both in the opposite direction from the landmark.

A third bearing will produce an even better fix. The most accurate results will come from using bearings close to ninety degrees apart, which isn't always possible. If bearings are very close together or a half-circle apart, the intersection won't be as precise.

Sometimes you may start out knowing nothing about

where you are except that you can identify one landmark. When you plot the bearing to it on the map, you
at least know that you are somewhere along that line.
By comparing the terrain and the map, you may then be
able to identify a second point of reference.

If the location you plot by triangulating doesn't make
sense with what you see around you, maybe:

- you read the compass wrong.

- you misidentified points you took bearings
on.

- you incorrectly transferred bearings to the
map.

What Are We Looking At?

If you know where you are, you can identify any visible
terrain feature, provided that it's on the map. If necessary, figure your location first by triangulation.

Take a bearing on the mystery landmark and plot it
from your spot on the oriented map *toward* the landmark.
Put one *back* corner of the base plate on your location
and pivot the whole compass until the needle and orienting arrow line up. Draw a line across the map along the
edge of the base plate and study the features it intersects.
One of them will be your landmark.

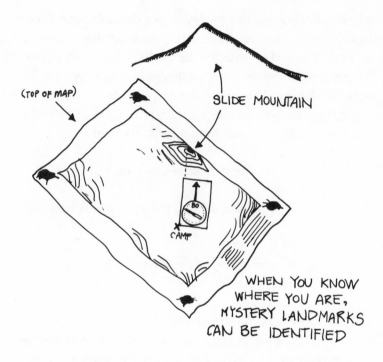

(TOP OF MAP)

SLIDE MOUNTAIN

80

CAMP

WHEN YOU KNOW
WHERE YOU ARE,
MYSTERY LANDMARKS
CAN BE IDENTIFIED

How can you remember whether to use a front or back corner of the compass base plate when you plot a bearing on the map? Use this simple formula: *You are at the back of the compass and *what you're looking at* is at the front. So, when you know only where you are, use the back corner; when you know only what you're looking at, use a front corner.

Going Somewhere You Can't See

You might want to travel to an unseen destination for the fun and adventure of it. Perhaps you'd like to spend a day exploring a lake that lies beyond the next group of low hills, or maybe you want to plot the route for a week-long cross-country ramble. The same map and compass skills applied in these activities can also be used in a genuine pinch, such as going for help when visibility is poor. The steps are:

1. Orient the map.

2. Mark your start and destination.

3. Choose the best route between them.

4. Measure the route bearings on the map.

5. Follow them.

Study the map to decide on the best actual route for getting to your destination. Now, on the oriented map, measure the bearing(s) along the course you choose.

Here's how. Place the compass on the map so that one side edge touches both your location and destination, with the direction-of-travel arrow pointing toward the goal. Hold the base plate steady on this line and turn the housing until the needle and orienting arrow line up. Draw the line between start and goal. Read the bearing where the direction-of-travel arrow intersects the dial (120 degrees in the drawing below of a bearing from Demaris Lake to Red Meadow). Don't turn the housing!

How do you get headed in the right direction? Load your pack, and fold the map with your travel area out for ready reference. Hold the compass horizontal in front of you with the first route bearing still set, and turn yourself and the compass until the needle and orienting arrow line up. You're pointed toward your destination—or first

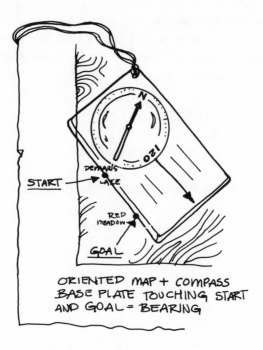

ORIENTED MAP + COMPASS
BASE PLATE TOUCHING START
AND GOAL = BEARING

leg of the route, if it consists of more than one bearing. You can now reach your goal by using the compass to get to intermediate landmarks along the way.

Occasionally you may find it necessary to hike in very bad visibility. There should be an absolutely compelling reason, for otherwise it's safest to wait for better conditions. Suppose you hiked cross-country over a notch in a ridge yesterday, making camp in a fine valley. This morning your friend took a bad fall on slippery rocks. Assessing the situation, you decide to go for help. The ridge is rugged, but you know the notch affords a good way over, and you could be back with help in a few hours . . . *if* you knew where the notch was! A thick fog covers everything beyond the valley floor.

But a compass works regardless of visibility, and can

help you out of this predicament. Orient the map, measure the bearing from camp to notch, and follow it by choosing intermediate landmarks that you can see. Write down the original bearing so you can use the back-bearing to get from notch to camp in case the fog is still heavy when you return. Even if each leg of the trip is only fifty yards long, this method of travel is much wiser than wandering totally disoriented in white-out weather.

Base Lines and Deliberate Error

The idea of hiking toward a base line works with just a compass and general knowledge of the area, but the possibilities are even broader with the added help of a map.

With map *and* compass you can travel toward a base line you can't see to take a bearing on, because you can "see" the road or river on the map and accurately measure its direction from you. If you had to, you could travel on this bearing even in poor visibility.

The procedure of using deliberate error can be done better with a map than with a compass alone; a map will provide a clearer idea of the destination and what sort of country you'll have to go through to reach the base line. You can use this idea to advantage in some off-trail ramblings, too. For instance: the map shows an intriguing small lake a couple of miles from base camp. The lake has an outlet stream that you can trace on the map for a considerable distance. If you set a course for the lake itself, you'd be mighty lucky to hit it exactly after a two-mile walk, and you could miss in the direction opposite the outlet. To be sure of ultimately finding the lake, aim instead for the creek, slightly downstream from the lake.

DELIBERATE ERROR AIMING FOR A LONG TARGET INSTEAD OF A SMALL ONE THAT'S EASY TO MISS.

Use this same method to return to camp near a baseline stream. Deliberately plan to hit it *upstream* from camp; then you'll know to travel downstream.

How far off should you aim in deliberate error? Far enough that your inevitable small deviations from a straight course won't matter.

BEARINGS AS BASE LINES. In places where a natural base line does not exist, you can *create* an abstract base line with a compass bearing measured from your starting point to some landmark—for instance, a distant peak. Another bearing to a second landmark fixes the point's exact location on the first bearing base line.

With the cross-bearings *written down* you're free to wander around the area as long as visibility allows for sighting on the landmarks you chose. As always, keep an alert eye out for weather changes! Say your explorations take you considerably east and south of camp. Sight on

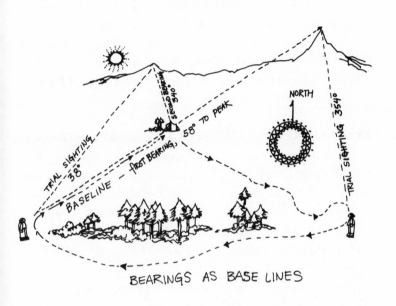

TRIAL SIGHTING 38°

SECOND BEARING 340

58° TO PEAK

NORTH

354°

BASELINE — FIRST BEARING

TRIAL SIGHTING 354°

BEARINGS AS BASE LINES

the first landmark peak. Your bearing of 354 degrees is way off the 58-degree reading you want, and it tells you the desired base line is much farther west. Start sighting again when you've moved some distance to the west; your bearing will read 58 degrees as soon as you reach the line.

Which way to turn? From there, sight on the second landmark. A trial bearing of 38 degrees says it was shot from west of the peak, but the 340-degree bearing from camp was taken from east of it. This tells you which way to walk along the base line (a "right turn" here). The second peak will eventually be on a bearing of 340 degrees, and if you haven't strayed off the first bearing base line, you should be very close to camp.

To avoid getting off course, remember to make use of intermediate landmarks along the bearing line, keep close track of deviations as you make them and correct for any detours as soon as possible.

BRACKETING: ANOTHER BASE-LINE SAFETY MEASURE.

When planning to return to a base line, do everything you can to assure that you'll be able to reach the particular *point* on the line you want. "Bracketing" that point with landmarks on either side is sometimes the best way.

You "mark" these enclosing points far enough apart on the base line so you'll be sure to reach it somewhere between them.

The brackets might be natural features along the line that you note from studying the map: "Camp lies at the base of the ridge, halfway between a notch to the north and the only treed gully to the south." Visible from a distance, brackets such as these make travel much easier and looser. There's no need to use compass bearings when you can sight the brackets frequently enough to keep headed in the right general direction. Keep in mind, though, that terrain features can sometimes disappear for a while, and that they might appear changed when viewed from different directions.

When your base line is a stream, note distinctive features a distance upstream and downstream from camp: "Twin waterfalls a quarter of a mile upstream, narrow cliff-lined gorge half a mile south."

For markers you might tie paper strips to trees along

the logging road where you left your car, or along the shore of a long lake, a mile or less each way from your destination. Markers of this kind should include notes about the direction of your goal, or you can make entries in your notebook when you place them: "Marker south from camp is on lone ponderosa; north marker on lodgepole pine."

Learning These Procedures

You can practice some basic map and compass operations even at home. Orient several maps of different declination until this fundamental process is automatic. Measure the bearings between a pair of points on an oriented map, and plot the best route by studying what the map indicates about the terrain along the bearing line. When you've run through this procedure several times, the different steps will begin to come easily.

Take map, compass and this book on a hike over familiar ground in clear weather. Take bearings on landmarks you know, then plot them on the oriented map. Move to another spot, orient the map again, measure and plot more bearings. By time to head home, you'll be friends with these routines.

When you have these basic procedures well in hand, try them in cross-country travel, nearby and in familiar territory. Measure the bearing on the oriented map to an easy off-trail goal—maybe a lake at the base of a cliff you can see from the trail, or a ridgeline pass that will offer a great lunchtime view. Carefully write down all the route-related clues you've discovered, in addition to the bearing, and go!

6

True Directions, or As the World Turns

There are a few instances when it's helpful to be able to measure and perhaps follow a **true direction,** a bearing measured using true north (remember, maps are laid out with the vertical grid lines running true north and south). If you want to know, for instance, which way is true east (90 degrees), a 90-degree bearing measured from magnetic north on the compass won't tell you. It would be off by the amount of your declination. Only if you were hiking somewhere along the line of zero-degree declination would true north and compass north be the same.

Measuring bearings that have to do with the sun calls for true directions also. The sun moves in relation to true directions; true north represents the endpoint of the axis on which the earth rotates. If you want to know where the sun will rise, you need to think in *true* directions because that's how the sun "thinks."

It's a fairly simple matter to adjust for this peculiarity and determine true directions. First, you need to know the magnetic declination for your hiking area. You'll find it at the bottom of the USGS topographic map, looking like this:

To Find True North

Turn the compass housing so that N lines up with the top, where the direction-of-travel arrow intersects the dial. Hold the compass horizontal in front of you and turn your body and the compass as a unit until the north-seeking end of the needle points *to your declination.* For areas with an easterly declination, that will be the number itself. For example:

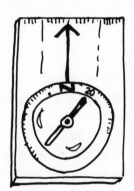

COMPASS ORIENTED TO TRUE NORTH IN AN AREA WITH A DECLINATION OF 20°E.

A westerly declination will be found left of N, so you must subtract its number from 360 degrees, which of course is the same as N. For instance: a hiker whose declination is 16 degrees west will turn until the compass needle lines up with 344 (360 — 16):

COMPASS ORIENTED TO
TRUE NORTH IN AN
AREA WHERE
DECLINATION IS 16°W.

You have now marked off the declination; the direction-of-travel arrow and N on the dial point to true north. You have oriented yourself so that N, E, S and W on the compass match true north, east, south and west in the actual landscape.

Following Other True Directions

Suppose a friend has told you about a good trail that is a quarter-mile true east of your camp. How do you get pointed in that direction? Turn the compass housing so that E (90 degrees) is at the top, lined up with the direction-of-travel arrow. Hold the compass horizontal in front of you and turn body and compass until the north-seeking end of the needle lines up with your declination. For the declinations in the previous examples, the compass will look like this:

COMPASS SET FOR TRUE EAST

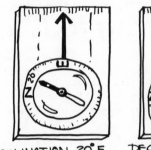 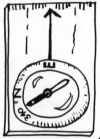

DECLINATION 20° E   DECLINATION 16° W

To head true east, follow the direction-of-travel arrow using landmarks along your destination line.

This procedure can be used to get yourself headed on *any true bearing*. Simply:

1. Turn the compass housing so the number of your chosen bearing lies at the top where the direction-of-travel arrow meets the dial.

2. Turn body and compass as a unit until the north-seeking end of the needle lines up with your declination.

3. The direction-of-travel arrow now points along your chosen bearing.

The next chapter deals with some of the time and direction clues we can get by observing the sun. Some of the procedures involve measuring true directions and will give you a very practical way to use the skill you just learned.

7
Looking to Nature for Help

So far we've been considering how to get around in the quiet places by using man-made tools: map and compass. But nature itself provides information to help us make our way. While nature's clues can give you very rough ideas about direction and time, they are better than no ideas in a pinch when you lack more accurate aids. And even if no genuine emergency arises, it's fun to practice these skills and comforting to know you can estimate direction based on where the sun should be at a given time of year or on recognizable star patterns and figure out the time of day from the sun's position.

Two basic kinds of information are constantly needed in making route-finding decisions: **direction** and **time.** The reasons for needing direction are obvious, but many people, accustomed to being able to extend daylight by the flip of a switch, underestimate the importance of time in planning their travels.

The length of day is crucial when your activities are tied to sun-time. Will you reach that off-trail goal before dark? How many miles can you realistically plan to cover on a late fall hike when the sun may be setting as early as six o'clock? And sunset, if you're deep in a canyon, will come much earlier for you than for the rim walker.

This section will cover several procedures for arriving at rough estimates of direction and time by observing natural elements. Should you need to make your way using *only* information gained in this fashion, accept that your travel paths must be conservatively chosen and will lack the precision of compass routes. Without a compass you can't take bearings and travel to unseen goals by using intermediate landmarks.

What *can* you do with clues about direction and time gained from nature? Aside from the fun and satisfaction of adding this source of information to your other sources, could you really make use of it in an emergency? Yes, as long as visibility is good enough to make sun clues available. Even on an overcast day a stick or knifeblade will often cast a faint shadow on a light surface such as paper or snow. Of course, in really poor visibility it's probably wisest to sit tight and await improved conditions or rescue.

Knowing what time it is without a watch (many people deliberately avoid using one, or you may lose or break yours) can help you judge whether to keep traveling, how far you can get, when it's time to stop and make camp, how much exploring time is left before you need to return to base camp.

What about direction? If your compass is lost or broken, how can you stay or get found?

From your knowledge of the area and your approximate location, decide which general direction is the best way out. A map simplifies this decision, but even if you don't have one there's quite a bit of information you probably *do* have:

- how far you've traveled.

- what direction you came from.

- base lines in the area.

- the general location of terrain to *avoid*, such as cliff systems, uncrossable streams, deep canyons, rugged mountains.

In the following problems, **knowing where the sun should be** makes it possible to use it as a guide for travel. Sometimes this is as simple as walking straight toward the sun, or always keeping it to one side of your travel line. In deciding where to move in relationship to the sun, you might want to draw a rough map or diagram which makes your situation easier to visualize.

Problem 1. I hiked cross-country about three miles south from an east-west base-line road, and now I need to return, but without the help of the compass I lost. It's about midmorning in late August, so the sun should be southeast of me in the morning and southwest in the afternoon (the sun's seasonal paths will be described later). To hike out north in the morning, I can aim generally opposite the sun and somewhat to the right, keeping it behind my *right* shoulder. When the sun is highest in the sky, my shadow will fall north. At that time I can try to spot some large landmarks to the north that could provide additional guidance. If I haven't reached the base line by the time the sun starts dropping from its highest position, then I should move along so that the sun is to the *left* and behind me as the afternoon progresses. This will keep me headed generally north.

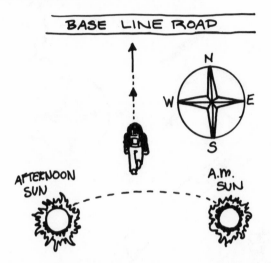

Problem 2. On a late December snowshoe trip I need to make my way out without a compass. There's a base-line ridge running north-south about a mile to the west. If I can get to the base of the ridge, I can follow it south to a highway. So I want to head *west.* In late December the sun's daily path is far to the southeast-southwest. It's afternoon, but with over two hours of daylight left it's reasonable to try for the ridge base. My line of travel should keep the sun in the area *between straight ahead and my left shoulder.* (See the illustration on page 98.)

The Sun, Direction and Time

Try to fix in your mind the sun's approximate path and its relative location from you at different times of the year. At home in the city, notice its rising and setting places as the months pass, and the changing amounts of sunlight

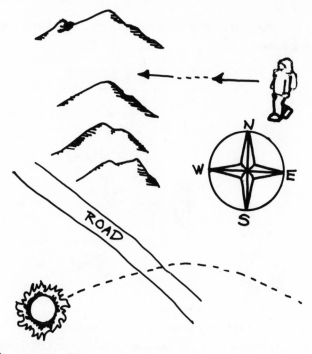

that come through your windows at different seasons. This will keep you aware of the sun's motions during your citybound times and reinforce the habit of noticing its location.

In the northern hemisphere the sun's path is generally south of us during fall, winter and spring. In summer the arc will be northeast to northwest.

Only twice each year does the sun cross the equator, making day and night of approximately equal length. These times—the equinoxes—occur about March 21 and September 22. Moving gradually northward from its spring equinox position, the sun takes three months to reach its extreme northerly path in late June. From its fall equinox path it drifts slowly southward for three months toward its extreme southerly path in late December. In late June the sun will rise northeast and set northwest; in late December its arc extends from southeast to southwest.

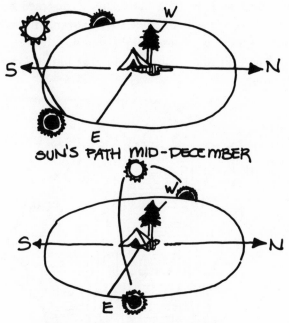

SUN'S PATH MID-DECEMBER

SUN'S PATH MID-JUNE

At any time of year, the sun is true south at its highest point (as is the moon). For someone at the center of his time zone (in an east-west sense), the sun is directly true south at noon standard time, and his shadow will point true north.

This varies a little with your position in your time zone. If you're east of the center, sun-events happen at an earlier clock time; west of the center, they happen later. Time zones are spaced at longitudinal intervals of approximately fifteen degrees around the globe. The sun moves fifteen degrees an hour, crossing one whole time zone.

Here's how this works out. If you're hiking near the eastern edge of your time zone, say 7 degrees east of its center, the sun will be true south seven fifteenths of an hour sooner, or twenty-eight minutes *before* noon standard time (it takes four minutes for the sun to move one degree).

North American time zones

A rough notion of **direction** can be had by the old stick-shadow method, based on the westward motion of the sun. This is most accurate around midday. Stand a straight stick at least two feet long upright in the ground (the longer the stick, the faster this works). Mark the tip of the shadow. In a few minutes, when the sun has moved west and the shadow has shifted noticeably eastward, mark the tip of the new one. Make one or two more markings as the shadow moves. A line connecting the marks will run east and west, with west being at your first marker. A line perpendicular to this one will run north and south. This method is rough; it produces a straight line only around mid-March and mid-September and arcs the rest of the time.

If you have a non-digital watch, it can be used with the sun for a rough direction estimate. Set your watch on standard time (move it back an hour if you're on daylight saving time) and face the sun. Hold the watch horizontal and point the hour hand at the spot on the horizon directly below the sun. South will be halfway between the hour hand and twelve o'clock. This method is based on the fact that the hour hand moves 30 degrees an hour, twice as fast as the sun.

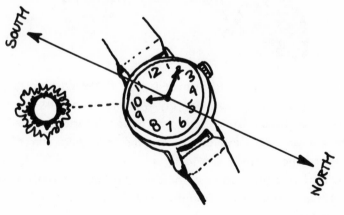

What matters to the outdoor traveler is not official sunset time, but **how much daylight is left** at his particular location. Use the following method in late afternoon to find out.

Fully extend your left arm in front of you with thumb pointed up, fingers extended together and palm angled toward you. Move your arm until the sun rests in the corner of the L formed by your palm and thumb. Now observe the vertical distance from there to the point on the horizon where the sun will disappear in terms of finger-widths (remember that the sun will continue to angle a bit to the right as it sets). Each finger-width represents about fifteen minutes of daylight, so if the distance is four fingers you have approximately one hour until the light dims and the air chills. If sunset is more than an hour away, you'll need to enlist the aid of your other hand.

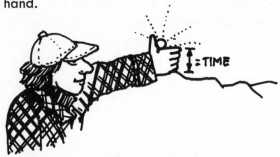

This same method can help you determine morning clock time if you know roughly when the sun rises where you are, didn't bring your watch and happen to sleep later than you planned to. Do the arm and sun trick toward the easterly sun to figure out how long it's been up and add that span of time to the time of sunrise to get the current hour. You may need to revise your hiking goal for the day!

Estimating Time by Sun Bearings

Based on the fact that the sun travels fifteen degrees an hour across the sky, a rough notion of clock time can be obtained by taking true bearings on the sun. This method is most accurate in the two-hour spans before and after noon, and even then may be off by up to thirty minutes. There are several complicating factors: often our horizon-to-horizon sky isn't an exact half-circle, and the sun doesn't make an arc directly overhead. But if you're hurrying to cross a glacier-fed stream before 11:00 A.M., as a trail log might suggest, this is better than no idea of time.

Even if there's no pressing reason, it's fun to estimate the time this way, and if you choose not to wear a watch, you'll still have a good general idea what time it is.

Remember that the sun is true south, or 180 degrees, at noon standard time in the center of your time zone. To roughly estimate clock time between mid-morning and mid-afternoon, take a true bearing on the sun:

> **1.** Point the direction-of-travel arrow at the spot on earth directly under the sun.

> **2.** Turn the compass housing until your declination lines up with the north-seeking end of the needle.

> **3.** Read the true bearing where the direction-of-travel arrow intersects the dial.

What time is it? Figure out the difference between this bearing and 180 degrees. If the bearing is *less* than 180, subtract it from 180. If it's *more*, subtract 180 from

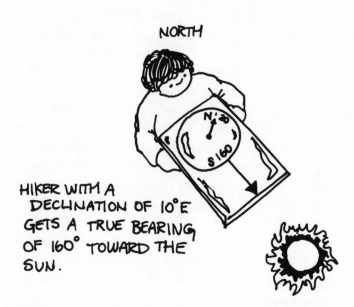

NORTH

HIKER WITH A
DECLINATION OF 10°E
GETS A TRUE BEARING
OF 160° TOWARD THE
SUN.

it. In the illustration, the hiker gets a difference of 20 degrees (180 — 160). Divide the difference by 15. For him, the sun is still 1⅓ hours away from its noon position (20 ÷ 15 = 1⅓), so clock time is roughly 10:40 A.M.

In another place with a declination of 10 degrees west, a hiker finds the sun on a bearing of 210 degrees. The sun has traveled 30 degrees past its noon position (210 — 180 = 30) and the time is therefore approximately 2:00 P.M. (30 ÷ 15 = 2).

These examples assume the hiker is at about the center of his time zone. That's close enough for this rough "clock." If you want more precision and enjoy fiddling, you can throw in a further adjustment. If you're hiking in an area *not* at the center, adjust the clock time estimate accordingly (four minutes for each degree you are off the center of the zone). East of the center, where sun-

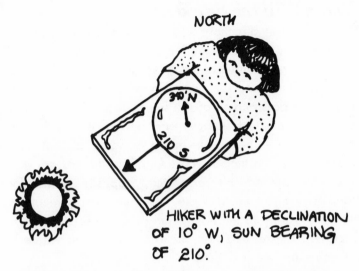

NORTH

HIKER WITH A DECLINATION
OF 10° W, SUN BEARING
OF 210°.

events happen earlier, *subtract* from the estimate; west of the center, *add* to it. (If you're not sure about your position in the time zone, look at the time zones map in your telephone directory.)

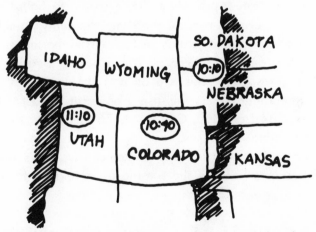

If a sun bearing yields the time estimate of 10:40, it would be adjusted to 10:10 at the eastern edge of the time zone or 11:10 at the western edge

Where Will the Sun Rise?

Measuring true directions has a very practical application that can add a bit of luxury to your camping. Remember Carrie, who wanted to set up her tent so she'd wake with the rising sun shining in the door? Carrie knew from her understanding of the sun's seasonal path that it rarely rises and sets exactly east and west; that its arc usually varies either to the north or south of that line, depending on the time of year. At all but the east-to-west times, the sun doesn't set exactly opposite in the sky from its rising place. If it did, we could simply measure the true bearing to the point where the sun sets and subtract 180 degrees (a half-circle) to figure out where it will come up the next day.

Because the sun's path will usually be either "above" or "below" the east-west line, you can estimate its rising point by taking a true bearing on its setting point and subtracting that number from 360.

Say it's late April when Carrie wants to figure out where the sun will rise. At that time the sun's path for the northern United States will be from northeast to northwest, and she's likely to get a setting bearing of 284 degrees or so. This is a bit north of west, and she can expect that the sun will rise a bit north of east. Subtracting 284 from 360, Carrie gets 76, the approximate *rising* bearing of the sun.

Here's how Carrie does it. Remember, she's using *true* bearings because the sun moves in relation to true directions, not magnetic.

> **1.** She points the direction-of-travel arrow at the place on the horizon where the sun will set.

2. She turns the compass housing until her declination (20 degrees east in this example) is at the north-seeking end of the needle.

3. Where the direction-of-travel arrow meets the dial, she reads the true bearing, 284 degrees.

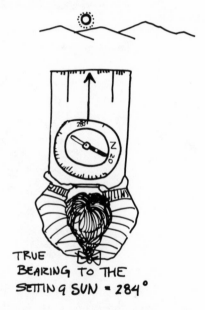

TRUE
BEARING TO THE
SETTING SUN = 284°

4. Carrie subtracts 284 from 360, getting 76.

5. She now turns the compass housing until the rising bearing of 76 degrees is lined up with the direction-of-travel arrow.

6. Holding the compass horizontal, she turns body and compass until the declination is again marked off by the needle's north-seeking end.

7. She has pointed herself at the sun's rising bearing, and looks up to find that point on the distant horizon. Looking around the camp-

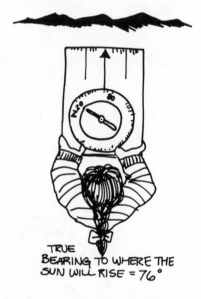

TRUE
BEARING TO WHERE THE
SUN WILL RISE = 76°

site, Carrie notes that a group of tall fir trees near the other tents will keep them in shade for an hour or more after sunrise, so she erects her shelter where there won't be any shadow-makers between her and the sun.

True direction to the rising and setting sun on the first day of each month for 40 degrees north latitude, an average for the United States. (The direction to the sun varies with your latitude.)

	rising	setting
January	121°	239°
February	113°	247°
March	100°	260°
April	84°	276°
May	70°	290°
June	67°	293°
July	59°	301°
August	66°	294°
September	79°	281°
October	94°	266°
November	109°	251°
December	119°	241°

The Night Sky

Nighttime hiking is almost never wise, but if you've lost your compass you can use the stars to figure out directions, mark them and make use of this information the next day.

Like the sun, stars rise in the east and set in the west, except for the stars which rotate around Polaris, the North Star, which never set.

Polaris, to the naked eye the only star which doesn't move, is never more than one or two degrees off true north. It's fairly bright, and most North Americans will find it about halfway between the northern horizon and the zenith (overhead).

You can locate Polaris in relation to either the Big Dipper (Ursa Major) or Cassiopeia (whose five brightest stars form a W). These constellations and the Little Dipper (Ursa Minor) all rotate counterclockwise around Polaris, which is the end star of the Little Dipper's handle. All three constellations can be seen year-round, so they're good direction-finders. (Most constellations disappear beneath the horizon at various times of the year because of the tilt of the earth's axis.)

Polaris is about halfway between the Big Dipper and Cassiopeia. A line drawn through the two outer stars of the Big Dipper's bucket and extended about five times the distance between them will reach Polaris.

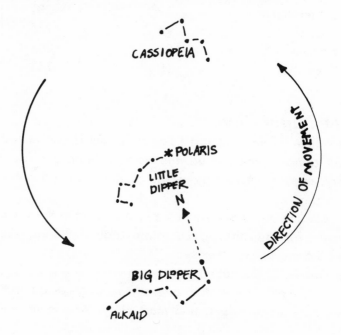

If the Big Dipper is hidden by clouds or a hill on your northern horizon, use Cassiopeia to locate Polaris. Roughly opposite the Big Dipper, its five brightest stars form a W, with the top always toward Polaris.

At least two other constellations can be used to find north. The top of Orion, a winter constellation in the northern hemisphere, is consistently toward the north, and so is the back of Leo.

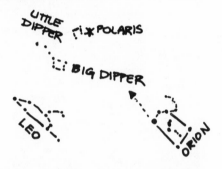

LEO'S BACK AND THE TOP
OF ORION POINT TOWARD NORTH.

If clouds or the view from your campsite thwart efforts to locate Polaris, try to find east. Watch the horizons and see where the stars are rising. A few minutes of patient observation will give you the answer. Once you've determined which direction is east, north is to your left.

Vegetation

Vegetation growth follows some *general* directional rules, but conditions such as local weather and the shape of the land are always complicating factors. Take general clues from observing the green things, but don't rely on them except as a last resort.

In the northern hemisphere, north and northeast slopes

get less direct sun in a day than south-facing ones and hence are cooler and damper. In general the vegetation on north-facing slopes is greener and richer, and snow and ice will last longer.

Does moss *really* grow mainly on the north sides of trees? Generally it may be thicker there, but you can find moss growing on any and all sides of trees because of the climate in a particular spot.

8

Route Planning

Where to Go?

Your first itch to explore an area might come from friends, an enticing description in an outdoor magazine, a hint from the outdoor-store clerk, or maybe from studying unknown territory on a map.

If there are regional offices for the Forest Service and Bureau of Land Management in your vicinity, pay them a visit. They can sell you maps and provide current information about the wild places they oversee. Because these agencies are trying to combat overuse of a few popular areas, they're glad to steer you toward fine spots that are less publicized.

Wilderness areas, the most use-restricted of our backcountry, are designated by Congress and found within publicly owned lands. The managing agency will be able to tell you which parts of a wilderness area are most frequented and which are likely to yield solitude.

Within each Forest Service region are anywhere from one to twenty national forests full of hikeable country. Each national forest has a supervisor's office (look in the phone book under United States Government, Department of Agriculture), and this is another source of ideas about where to go. In addition to maps, you can sometimes obtain detailed trail logs (mile-by-mile descriptions) to help plan your trip.

Your state may have extensive forest lands under its supervision, with offices that can suggest places to wander.

Along with maps of your trip area, find out if there are any use restrictions and if a permit system is in force. You need to know if the number of campers is limited at a lake you want to visit. Sometimes whole areas are temporarily closed due to high fire-danger levels. A bridge on your route may have been washed out. Your favorite alpine camping area may be restricted, cordoned off and replanted in an effort to restore trampled vegetation. The local ranger or his counterpart is usually the best source of current information about road and trail conditions and the like. Some outdoor stores post current national forest ranger district reports.

In settlements near your trailhead you can often ferret out verbal descriptions and suggestions from the townsfolk. Frequently this is sound and helpful, and leads you to some gem of a place you would otherwise have missed. But weigh this kind of advice carefully. All too often a description of the trail and country comes from the fond but distant memory of one who was last there twenty years ago.

Bookstores and outdoor stores carry a proliferation of hiking guidebooks which can supply enough trip ideas to fill every remaining weekend of a long and vigorous life. These books give abundant details about the hikes proposed, including which USGS maps cover the area, how to get to the trailhead, hiking times, available water and, sometimes, interesting geologic and historical background. Indeed, such descriptions are often so vivid that you can almost count on finding any publicized trails crowded with other folk who've succumbed to the printed lure.

How Can You Avoid the Crowds?

Plan your trips for times other than weekends, holidays and the peak hiking season. Go to spots more than five miles from a busy trailhead, or enter a popular area from the least used side, away from major population centers. Choose areas away from tourist attractions, big campgrounds and major highways—a few miles of unpaved road to a trailhead deter a lot of people! Avoid lakes easily reached by trails.

Stay off major, well-publicized trails such as the Pacific Crest Trail and the Appalachian Trail, at least at peak times. Explore lesser-known secondary trails. Include some cross-country travel in your route; you can be all alone just out of sight of a heavily used trail, because most hikers stick to trails.

Detailed Map Study

Take a good close look at the topographic map *before* you pack up to hit the trail. It can give you all manner of information related to planning an itinerary.

Even for a hike done entirely on trails, a map helps.

■ The map will preview just where the trail goes and show some of the treasures and obstacles along the way—a great ridgetop view, a challenging water crossing.

■ Elevations can tell you where you might encounter lingering snows in early summer, and where a late October walk could include dusting by early snowfall.

■ The patterns of contour lines will tell how steep a stretch of trail will be, how hard the climb between two points, and help you estimate travel time and set realistic goals.

■ You can figure out water sources from their symbols and the season of your hike, so you'll carry enough, but not too much, water —one quart weighs two pounds!

■ A look at the topography may suggest special travel equipment you'll need: ropes to aid in difficult water crossings, ice axes for a high exposed pass on an early season trip, tennis shoes for fording streams.

■ Knowing a buggy swamp lies on your route, you can plan to travel past in the cool morning hours.

■ A map will alert you to glacier-fed streams that should be crossed early in the day before they swell.

■ Map study provides a view that walking the trail can't: a look at the *whole* piece of land the trail is just one part of.

Other Planning Matters

What's the likely travel time for each leg of your proposed route? On moderate trails, carrying an average load, you may travel about a mile and a half an hour. Steep walking is much slower, of course. How far or fast you move is an individual matter best determined by your own experience; this has to do not just with the kind of country you're traveling over, but with such factors as weather, group pace and the purpose of your trip.

Remember that the first day's goal should be conservative. Loads are heaviest, hikers possibly out of shape and acclimatizing to higher elevations. Always allow for a margin of time and energy reserve. If you are set on camping at a special spot and reach it two hours sooner than expected, you can always use the extra time exploring. But it's bad news to trudge on with fading light and energies toward a rigidly held goal.

When you're sizing up possible routes, consider what the terrain will be like at this particular time of year. For instance, a large stream-threaded meadow at 6200 feet will be swampy and buggy for several weeks after the snows recede, but in late summer and early fall will make an idyllic base camp. In winter its many streams could make for slow roaming, since cold-season travelers don't wade barefoot and water crossings can be major logistical challenges.

A frequent seasonal problem is the availability of water. I learned one very long and thirsty late summer day how much care is called for in map-scouting the water supply. Assuming there was water in the small ponds shown high on a long ridge, I carried almost none. To camp near water that night, I hiked several miles farther than originally planned.

Planning Cross-Country Travel

Map-scouting is twice the fun when you're ready to forsake the well-trod paths. Test your map and compass skills and build confidence with easy hikes under favorable circumstances. Make your first off-trail trips during good weather, in varied terrain with distinctive landmarks that provide ready route-finding clues.

How about a weekend trip on a route that uses trails part of the time but also takes you into easy trackless terrain? Or a base camp near a trail, with cross-country daytime probes in different directions? You might try cross-countrying in an area enclosed by a loop trail or a valley between two ridges. Maybe there's a lake whose outlet you could follow for a mile or two until it crosses a trail.

A sense of the Big Picture is always important to a wilderness traveler, but it is absolutely crucial to one who leaves the trails. Because the land itself is your guide, "losing" landmarks in poor visibility has more impact than it does on the hiker who can still see his path and trail signs. It's essential that the cross-country walker be constantly aware of the *total* scene and his place in it. Then, if the larger picture shrinks in a fog or white-out, he can alter course appropriately and in an informed way.

Prior map study should include looking for possible alternate routes and base-line features which could provide a way out if the need arose.

You'll need to estimate mileage yourself for the legs of a cross-country trip, since the map won't supply it in neat figures along a trail line. A map measurer rolled along your route will give a rough estimate. For steep country, increase that figure by 15–20 percent to get a more realistic notion of how far you'll walk. The map's red land survey lines can give you a rough idea, too. Each time you cross one section, you've moved about a mile horizontally. If your route winds around a lot, lay a piece of string along it, then stretch the string out along the map's bar scale.

Cross-country hiking is usually slow, but it isn't necessarily difficult going. You might travel through mature forests with little undergrowth, along a gentle ridge above timberline, across an open desert. In planning a trip, however, keep your goals conservative as to time and mileage; this will eliminate pressures that can nudge you into unwise choices as you travel. Cross-country can be great fun, but it may not go as expected—and the unpredictability is one of its appeals. You should have slack in both time and energy to allow for unexpectedly slow or difficult parts of your journey.

One factor that's crucial to an off-trail hiker is that the surface cover on white unforested areas of the map is often a mystery until you actually see the land. And what covers the ground directly affects the person who traverses it without benefit of trails. Ground surface or cover, combined with the shape of the land, determines the ease or difficulty of travel through it.

A flat area might be dotted with scratchy sagebrush. A formidably steep slope could have a new trail that goes right to the top—good reason to gather all possible current information—or it could be clothed in scree (small, loose rock) that makes for a slow climb up but an easy, fast descent. Talus (larger rocks) might either slow you down considerably or be easily negotiated by boulder-hopping.

You've picked the area and some particular spots you want to visit. How do you decide on a route? A basic rule is to *pick an energy-efficient course.* First plot the straight course between points, then study the terrain for the best way. Realize that the nearest, most direct route is often neither easiest nor best. Skirting a big brushy flat or going around the head of a tangled ravine may increase the distance but decrease the time. Avoid fighting your way along brushy stream banks, slogging through swamps, climbing and descending slopes. Go around obstacles such as vast areas of wind-downed timber or dense scrub.

Make use of the lay of the land rather than superimpose a rigid, straight course over it. If you decide to depart from the original bearing line, take advantage of natural routes such as draws, gentle slopes and clearings shown on the map. Plot bearings for short legs of the hike if they are at all unclear. Move along at the same elevation, or "contour," around hills in your path instead of going up and down simply to maintain a bearing.

Consider whether slopes face north or south. Depending on the season, you'll want to avoid much travel on north-facing slopes where lingering snows or thicker undergrowth would make the going more difficult.

When picking your course, take both a short- and long-range view of the options. The way that looks easiest in its early stretches may get you into problems later on. When possible, aim for a large or long destination such as a ridge, stream or long lake instead of a point. And use intermediate goals as checkpoints along the way; the risk of missing your destination increases with the distance traveled.

When It's Over

You can learn a great deal about route-finding with each cross-country trip. After it's over, retrace on the map your actual route, evaluating how the trip went and learning from both your successful choices and mistakes. Challenge and skill-sharpening are among the delights of off-trail travel.

9

How to Stay Found

With four miles and an elevation loss of 1600 feet to go, a friend and I savored a coming-off-the-ridge view of several lakes which lay at the base of the mountain. This was our fourth and last day of sampling part of the Pacific Crest Trail which traverses Mount Jefferson and Three-Fingered Jack in the Oregon Cascades. This year a major rerouting of a section had been completed, taking travelers high across the side of Jack rather than through lower lake basins suffering from years of heavy use.

Rounding a turn at an easy clip, we stopped abruptly and blinked. A group of college kids huffed and puffed up the ridge, toting a rubber raft, a six-pack of beer and little else! Without a map, they had started up this sparsely signed new PCT thinking they were headed for the lakes; in reality the closest water was ten tough miles from the trailhead.

Bartering map for a couple of beers, we helped them sort out their choices: a long backtrack or a shorter but tougher cross-country stint. In either case, a day of gentle lazing in the boat was not to be.

Why Do People Get Lost?

Rare is the hiker who has never been at least temporarily confused, unsure of his location if not lost. When people get lost, usually one or more of these reasons is involved:

- They don't know the territory, and don't do the map homework needed to start with a mental picture of the area.

- Their knowledge of the route isn't current enough; trailheads and access roads change, trails are rerouted or cease to be maintained.

■ They rely on the navigational know-how of a companion who is in the process of getting lost himself.

■ They travel without a map because the route seems obvious, a sin that casual day strollers are guilty of more often than overnight walkers.

■ They daydream and miss junctions or wander off on animal trails.

■ They rely on their nonexistent "sense of direction," even trust instincts over compass.

■ When adverse circumstances enter the picture—deteriorating weather and visibility, fatigue, flagging spirits and dulled awareness —they charge ahead anyway.

The many specific things you can do to increase your chances of staying found can be grouped according to the places you consider them:

■ before you leave home.

■ at the trailhead.

■ on the move.

■ around camp.

Staying Found Starts at Home

Head for your trip with a happy body and a brain ready to function efficiently. If you are taxed by lack of sleep, a bad cold, a hangover or a recent bout with flu, your best route-finding equipment (**you!**) is weakened before you're out the door.

Be sure you understand the rudiments of map and compass use *before* your trip. Applying and firming up these skills in the field will be much easier if you don't have to start from scratch. Be sure to *pack* map and compass, along with a pencil and paper for making notes on your route, plotting bearings and leaving emergency messages.

Study recent maps of the area to get as complete a mental picture as possible. Look at topographic maps for information about the planned route: its direction, elevation changes, landmarks you should see as the hike progresses. But go beyond the narrow aisle your trail occupies to get a feel for the Big Picture, the general lay of the land. This increases your range of alternatives once you're out there and could be helpful if you need to depart from your original plan. Are there any big baseline features such as a river, a ridge, a road? What directions do they run? Where are they in relation to your route? Consult a road map for clues about the surrounding country that could be useful in an emergency. Where are nearby towns and roads? How far away? In which direction?

Augment map study with information about current trail conditions and routes from others who've been there recently, up-to-date hiking guidebooks and a call or letter to the local ranger or his equivalent. Lingering snow may still cover the trail on the highest section of your planned hike; the first mile may have been rerouted because of overuse. It's better to know about changes such as these *before* you're wandering around trying to figure out what happened and where you are.

Without fail, even for a day hike, **leave a written itinerary** with some responsible person (who likes you). Should you run into trouble, this one act could save crucial hours or days. If you are lost, feeling assured that someone knows where to look and will soon be searching for you can keep panic in check. Leaving an itinerary is doubly important if you will be hiking cross-country.

In addition to *telling* your friend where you plan to travel and showing him on the map, *write it out.* In an emergency the brain often fails us—"Was it Devil's Peak or Angel's Peak they were going to climb?" Your note should include:

- names and emergency telephone numbers for group members (relatives or neighbors, for example).

- description and location of car(s).

- departure and expected return times.

- route, with likely campsites.

- alternate route and the circumstances under which you'd use it.

- list of visually distinctive equipment.

- whom to contact (county sheriff, district ranger or other rescue personnel) if you're overdue and how long to wait before calling for rescue. (When you return, be sure to check in so your friend knows you're back!)

Group size has a bearing on staying found. Do you plan to hike alone or with companions? Although solo hiking may sometimes be your choice, recognize that your chances of getting lost are usually much greater alone, and act accordingly. Since there is no one to correct route-finding mistakes when you travel alone, use extreme care in planning and following your route.

On the other hand, an unmanageably large group can get strung out and lose someone who lags behind, goes off the trail for a bit or stops to smell the flowers. The family-sized group that the Forest Service now recommends for low ecological impact also makes sense for staying found.

At the Trailhead

Review road and topographic maps to fix in your mind a picture of the area. Orient the map, identify prominent landmarks and their directions from the trailhead. Note the compass bearing for the first stretch of trail. These bits of information could help you get back to your starting point.

If for some reason you decide at this point on a route change (perhaps car trouble on the way has trimmed available walking time), try to call home. If that's not feasible, at least leave a note on the dashboard indicating the change.

Some people advocate always leaving an itinerary note with the car telling where you'll be and your departure and return times. Unfortunately, trailhead vandalism is not unheard of these days, especially at very popular takeoff points. To announce your length of absence could sometimes invite trouble, so weigh that possibility.

On the Move

Keep map and compass handy so you can get at them without removing your pack—you'll use them more often. Your shirt or parka pocket might be the place, or an outside pocket within reach on your pack. If your pack doesn't have this feature, you can easily sew on a simple map pocket. Some folks like to wear a small beltpack

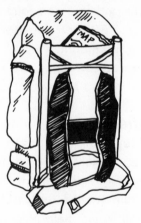

which houses items for use while traveling, including map and compass. It's a good safety measure to attach a cord to your compass and maybe run it through a buttonhole or around your belt. If skies are damp, be sure your map is protected from moisture in some way or your destination could disappear in a soggy fold! A pencil and paper should also be close at hand.

If group members have varying levels of route-finding skills, the more experienced navigators should use the opportunity to train others. *Everyone* needs to be an active route-finder, not just the first person in line or the one who has logged the most miles. Even a conscientious leader can miss a turn.

Is this the trail? Trails are marked in various ways. **Blazes** are carved from tree bark about four to eight feet off the ground in the shape of a diamond, a T, a

dotted i or something similar. You'll usually find a blaze on both the coming and going sides of trees, which are blazed at close enough intervals so you can spot the next one without moving far. A few cautions about blazes:

- Old blazed trees fall.

- Trees sometimes blaze themselves when one falls against another.

- Occasionally lost hikers carve blazes that might later confuse your situation.

On some trails you may find small **metal plates** with a trail symbol, instead of or in addition to blazes.

Cairns, or "ducks," are man-made piles of rock which mark routes above timberline, through meadows and in other unclear or treeless spots. Sometimes those at high elevations are swept away by avalanches; if you find a damaged cairn, try to rebuild it.

Trails are usually "brushed out" to a height of about eight feet. If you examine the trees on both sides of a trail you'll frequently find neat man-made **prunings** where limbs that would have stuck out into the path were trimmed. A saw or axe leaves a smooth, even cut; when an animal chews or pulls a branch off, the scar is jagged or uneven.

A **worn tread** itself is the trail evidence most often relied on, but the day is bound to come when you wonder if you've strayed onto an *animal* trail. The worn track is still there, but things don't feel quite the same as on a people trail. Deer trails are much narrower—about the width of your spread hand. Where logs lie across man's paths, he usually cuts through or moves them aside. Deer move easily over such obstacles. You'll probably need to duck to avoid brush and limbs which clear a deer's back easily.

An elusive trail on a slope will sometimes become clear if you look for the **terracing effect** where the path was cut into the hillside. If your travels take you on trails overgrown by brush, a bit of ground-level searching may disclose the path itself, free of greenery. Compacted earth takes a while to bounce back to a natural vegetation pattern.

Trail signs made of wood can be reduced to an unreadable state by vandals or gnawing critters, flattened by snow or carried off. I've seen junction signs turned the wrong way, like street signs after Halloween. Mileages on signs should be accepted as rough estimates; trust your map more for this information. There are plenty of reasons to have more than trail signs in your repertoire of route-finding aids!

Be particularly alert in circumstances where it's easy to lose the trail—reentering the trees after crossing a clearing; going back and forth over streams in a lush draw or a canyon bottom; early season hikes before the trail-clearing crew has been through and while snow patches may still cover an occasional stretch.

The key to knowing where you are is constant awareness.

What kind of terrain are you passing through? How is the landscape changing as you travel? Are you moving up a valley, traversing a ridge line between two watersheds, skirting the base of a massive butte, paralleling a tributary to its junction with another stream?

Think of the landscape as a whole, fitting in new features as they come into view and as you anticipate them from frequent map checks. Break out of the tunnel-vision that a trail and rhythmic footfall ahead can induce. **Look everywhere!** Notice close and distant landmarks, thinking about how they would look from other directions. Frequently **look back** where you came from, since that view is different and you may need to retrace your steps. Pay special attention to crucial junctions and turns.

Maintain constant orientation so that you are never unsure of where you are. Every fifteen minutes or so (more frequently in cross-country travel) match map and landscape, taking compass bearings if visual inspection alone doesn't yield a solid comparison. Pull out the map every time you reach a pass, junction or new view, and wherever you have the slightest uneasiness about your location.

Keep track of what direction you're moving in, how far you've come and approximate travel times. Be aware of changes in direction, always thinking of your progress through the landscape: "After a quarter-mile of going west toward Shelf Rock, we turned north and are now paralleling the valley floor about a third of the way up its east wall, heading for Goat Pass."

A landmark isn't just an impressive peak; it is anything you can note and recognize later—a meadow, trail, cairn, remains of a shelter, gully, distinctively shaped butte, saddle between two peaks. Even a bearing to the sun at a certain time can be considered a landmark, since you could use that information along with other clues to establish your location later. In thick woods, don't count on trees as landmarks, even oddly shaped or large ones. Instead, use things external to the woods: a river, distant peak, ridge, the shape and slope of the land.

If landmarks aren't visible because of bad weather or darkness, then reliance on map and compass is especially crucial. Don't stay uneasy about where you are for more than a few minutes. If you're that unsure, better to sit tight until visibility improves than to compound your dilemma by uninformed travel.

Whom can you trust? Sometimes your instincts about direction will conflict with what the compass says, even to the point of being totally opposite. **Believe your compass** —*after* ruling out attraction by nearby metal and checking with other compasses in the group. Unlike migrating birds, human wanderers have no internal compass. We can work at developing a sense of direction, but mainly it will come from the continued careful observation of natural phenomena—vegetation patterns, the sun's position and so on. Hone your observations by guessing which way is true north when your crew stops to rest.

The very types of terrain and weather that are easy to get lost in can also lull a hiker into daydreams. When flat, featureless country, a fogged-in tunnel of a path or dense woods are your trail lot for very long, your awareness can quietly click off without your noticing. Suddenly —as when driving across a desert on a hot day—you wake up and wonder how long you've been on automatic pilot and whether you passed that turnoff. The country you've come through during the lapse has left you with no route-finding clues; part of your equipment was shut down.

When traveling cross-country, and if your route is unclear or complex for any reason, *always* whip out that pad and pencil and make notes or even draw a map of your progress. Include landmark bearings, both ahead and behind, and travel times between points. Check off points on the map as you pass them, noting the time.

If you ever feel you must mark your trail in order to find the way back—as on an overgrown trail in a fog or in some cross-country rambling—*don't* wound the trees with blazes. Instead, tie on strips of colored crepe or toilet paper, which will last long enough to guide you out but not much longer. On the way out, remove your markers.

Keep all members of your group within earshot of one another, and within sight if you're traveling off-trail. Regroup at junctions and at any confusing or crucial points. Anyone who needs to stop or leave the trail should tell

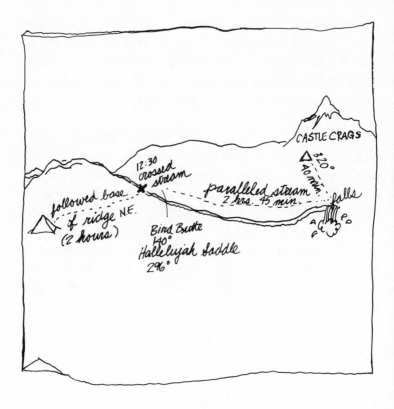

someone else. It's easy to go ten yards into woods and lose your bearings, then head away rather than toward the trail.

Stay in good shape to ensure that your powers of observation and judgment will operate well. When fatigue sets in, it's time for a renewing halt. Dehydration can dull the mind long before you realize what has happened. Other physical problems can crowd your head. A hiker preoccupied with an untended blister or ill-fitting pack won't pay much attention to staying found.

There's no substitute for **active judgment** about a

hike and all the factors affecting it—weather, how the group is doing, whether your pace matches what you anticipated, unexpected problems with gear, injuries and so on. Be flexible enough to make changes if circumstances so dictate, rather than rigidly pushing on toward the original goal along the path you planned. That may have been great on paper, but it isn't worth the price you could pay in safety and comfort. Sometimes, turning back in the face of deteriorating weather or serious illness is the best choice. The country will be there for your next try.

If you make changes in your itinerary it's wise and sometimes possible to leave a note in a prominent spot, especially if you're alone.

> *A friend and I found such a message on a late fall hike. All day we had seen one set of large bootprints ahead, with dog tracks trotting faithfully alongside. Tucked in among the rocks of a junction cairn near camp that night we found this note in a plastic bag: "Oct. 23, 1977. If you find this—I'm hiking alone from Frog Camp to Willamette Pass and am making a route change here. Instead of staying on the PCT to Island Meadow, I'm taking the trail from here to Horse Lake and Sunset Lake, to rejoin the PCT just north of Island Meadow. I expect to reach Willamette Pass Oct. 28. Please notify the proper authorities. Thanks. [Name and address.]" When we got home the next day we relayed his message to the district ranger and wrote the mystery traveler to say we'd found his*

note. Had his friends reported him overdue, his foresight would have given searchers a tremendous edge.

Around Camp

As you approach your home-for-a-night and soon after you drop packs, cast a careful roving eye on the surroundings. Map and compass in hand, compare what you see with its topographic picture.

What is the shape of the land? Where is camp in relation to the largest peaks around? Are there any distinctive features you could spot if you wandered out of sight of camp? A rock outcropping? Cliffs? A group of unusual snags? A break in the ridge line just west? If you are near a stream, note something distinctive a short distance away both upstream and downstream. Anything visible from a short distance will help. A friend once found his way back to camp in a huge canyon by heading for a big white blotch he had noticed on the wall above camp—a wood-rat urinating station.

By making this mental inventory of guides toward home (sometimes you might also want to jot a few notes in your pad), you are free to go exploring with an easy mind.

What to Do If You're Lost

Lost is too strong a label for those inevitable moments of disorientation or confusion, or for the many times when you don't know your exact location but don't feel lost at all.

Really lost is the predicament you can't work your way through in a few minutes, the situation that calls for resourcefulness and positive thinking. Few backpackers get really lost, unless they are extremely careless. And even being really lost rarely ends in tragedy. It may mean a day or two of discomfort while you await rescue— *unless* you lose your head and make things worse.

The greatest danger in being lost lies not in the weather or the country, but in giving way to fear and panic. Keep cool, calm and confident that you'll soon get found either by yourself or by others. A relaxed mind is better than a packful of emergency gear; remind yourself that most lost travelers either find their way or are found within two or three days. Remember that itinerary you left?

If you think you are lost, *stop!* Sit down, calm down. Control fear so you can think clearly. Keep the group together. Look around. Yell, or better yet, blow a whistle. You can blow a whistle a lot longer than you can yell, with less energy, and the sound carries better. Listen for an answer; three is a distress signal, two a response.

With oriented map at hand, pool all the information you have. Where were you last sure of your location? How long ago? If you've kept track of your progress you have at least a vague idea of your general location. After all, the top speed of a foot traveler can't take him very far off base very fast. Look at the country around you and examine the map for likenesses to the shapes and features you see.

Think back over the country you covered since your last confirmed location. You may decide you can retrace your steps in a relatively short time. If this is the action you take, mark the "lost" spot and take your pack with you. *Never* abandon your survival gear.

Look for prominent peaks, drainages, ridges, open areas. Use care and caution; wishful thinking can lead to a hasty misidentification of what you see. Even if you can take only one bearing to a known feature, remember that puts you *somewhere* on a line. Thinking of your rate of travel and last known location, you can probably estimate your position on the line by comparing the landscape around you with the map. If you sight *two* known landmarks, you're not lost at all!

If the spot where you stopped doesn't offer a view of the surrounding area, mark it with a cairn or with toilet paper and seek a nearby high place, taking your pack with you. But don't risk injury by climbing a cliff or tree; being lost is enough to deal with. You may be lucky enough to top a rise and find a bench mark with a printed elevation. That rise will most likely be marked on your map. This higher view will usually tell you where you are.

If it doesn't, return to the marked spot and make short straight-line probes in different directions (gear with you), always coming back to the center. In *all* your searching, eyeball every tree and rock for evidence. You may stumble onto a section corner marker, if not a blaze or trail sign.

Is there a base line you could head for? Consider the kind of terrain and probable distance to be negotiated before you would reach it. Remember that cross-country travel is usually slower than trail walking. If the base line isn't a quick or easy way out, at least it is a possible way. There may not be enough light left today, but perhaps tomorrow you could make it.

Sift all the evidence and don't travel unless you're sure of where you're going and there's plenty of daylight left. Don't follow a stream; many lead away from civilization rather than toward it. Resist the temptation to keep moving in the dark or in poor visibility. Getting hurt—cliffs, holes, creeks to fall in—could make getting out even harder. If you do decide to move, leave a note giving your departure time, bearing and destination.

Whatever actions you take while lost, conserve your energy for the cold and dark hours and the indeterminate interval until you are found. If you wear yourself out trying to get found, the possibility of trouble increases markedly. You can't function in a strong and wise way, and are much more vulnerable to hypothermia if things turn cold, wet and windy.

Two hours of daylight left and no good clues. Time to settle in for the night. Make shelter in a protected spot, get water and lots of firewood. Don't fret if your food supply is skimpy; most of us could survive on our fat reserve for a long time. Water, however, is *vital*. A day without it will strongly affect most body systems; much longer guarantees serious trouble.

If settling in means you move away from a cold but exposed place, first put a visible marker there. A bright piece of clothing or an X of stones could attract attention.

Your shelter may be just a windbreak rigged from a poncho if you are on a day jaunt without full gear. If you have *nothing* to work with, look for natural materials such as logs, large boulders, slabs of bark, boughs (an

emergency is the only justifiable reason for cutting them).
A tree-well can be the start of a serviceable shelter. Unless the country is tinder-dry, build a fire. Huddle for
warmth. Keep thinking about where you might be; you
may get ideas to act on in the morning. Continue signaling at intervals.

In the morning, assess the situation again and decide
whether to move—only on a *known* line to a *known*
destination—or stay put and await rescue. If you elect
to stay, you can help searchers by getting out in the open,
building a smoky fire, and blowing your whistle periodically. The hard-to-find person is the one who crashes
blindly on in a panic, depleting his energy as he goes.

After You're Found Again

Learn from your mistakes. Analyze what happened and
why. Think what you could have done differently to avoid
getting into trouble. This kind of careful retrospection
will fix in your mind how crucial small errors can be. You
may even discover some persistent patterns in your way-finding habits that keep getting you into jams.

In these examples of painful bits of learning from my
more careless days, hindsight was a good teacher.

> *The last day of a ski outing was marked by
> lousy visibility, so we were traveling entirely
> by close attention to the map and following
> short compass bearings. We turned south too
> soon, and realized our error after about ten
> minutes of unplanned downhill travel into a
> creek drainage. We elected to continue in
> this direction, a choice which booked us for
> several exhausting and sometimes risky hours*

traversing a steep wooded hillside above the creek, frequently carrying our skis. It would have been much safer and easier in the long run to correct our mistake, climbing back to the original elevation as soon as we discovered our error.

On our first venture into the high desert Steens Mountain country of southeast Oregon, a friend and I learned why responsible, successful foot travelers use topographic maps. Relying on a planimetric map and verbal descriptions from the locals ("It will all unfold like a map as you climb!"), we couldn't find a crucial pass. Altering plans, we worked our way out of one canyon and found a narrow rim separating it from its neighbor. We had scrambled part-way down the next canyon wall, much steeper, when darkness forced us to bivouac. Sleeping fitfully, we didn't know if or how we could get off the wall next morning. (We did.)

The lessons to be learned through post-adventure analysis add to your stock of way-finding skills.

10
Teaching Kids to Stay Found

In hiking with your offspring, a major concern is to nourish in them the same "staying found" skills you use yourself. Of necessity, young kids start out as passive travelers relying on the knowledge and authority of adults. If you succeed in implanting just one small "staying found" skill on each outing, your child will eventually become an active route-finder, staying found because of things he knows and does of his own volition.

First, concentrate on teaching kids **what to do if they suddenly feel lost**: Stop!

If you can't figure out where you are in a few minutes, then make lots of noise. Wait to be found. A whistle around a youngster's neck is a great comfort to both whistler and whistlee. Be firm in insisting it is not a toy, but for emergency use *only*.

Toddlers are adept at slipping out of sight in a blink of the most vigilant parent's eye. As you hike, this youngster may be riding in a kiddy-carrier most of the time, but when he's on his feet around camp you can easily be distracted for a second, and that's all his disappearing act takes. A clanky bell pinned to the back of your little one's jacket could help you find him before he gets far.

At the start of each hiking season, review with kids the basic staying found techniques you've already imparted. Don't assume they'll remember from year to year. This review won't hurt you either.

Make sure kids follow this safety rule: Let someone else know if you need to sit and rest or if you go off the trail for any reason. Encourage them to call you on it if *you* abuse this rule.

Set and enforce camp activity boundaries. Don't, however, assume they'll always be heeded. A young child usually gets lost in the process of satisfying his curiosity about things—chasing after a butterfly or squirrel, following a tiny stream, climbing over a rockpile to see what's in the cracks or on the other side. He hasn't yet developed an "adult" sense of insecurity about where he is or where he's going, so he doesn't naturally note landmarks or his place among them.

Even with fairly old children, insist they do their exploring in sight of an adult or at least tell one exactly where they'll be.

Kids' early trips afoot are best taken in territory you're familiar with—and not in a jumbled confusion of forested low hills or a featureless, flat place, both of which are easy to get lost in.

The small and close things of the world impress and intrigue a child, not the large-scale grandeurs we adults are awed by. A tiny waterfall you can crawl behind will win out over one four hundred feet high across the valley. You can build on this fact of life when nurturing the incipient route-finder in your child. Take advantage of his unquenchable thirst for small details—a person can't notice too many—and at the same time help him progress to noticing ever larger features of the land you're passing through. "This river is big because of all these little streams that feed it." (Point out the blue lines on the map.)

"This little snowbank hasn't melted yet because the sun never shines right on it. It's the same with that big hill. On the south side the snow has melted; on the north side it's still there."

Frequently, and in as many clever ways as you can dream up, be a model of constant awareness.

■ At rest stops and again at camp, play this game. "Look all around you, see as much as you can, big and little things. Is there water anywhere? Trees? Meadows? Hills? Cliffs? Where is the sun? Now close your eyes and talk about this place." Kids will soon try to outdo each other in the amount of detail their word pictures include.

■ Show kids how to recognize signs of a trail: blazes on trees, rock cairns, pruned branches, the worn path. Make a game of being first to spot the next blaze.

■ As your hike progresses, point out a few plant features peculiar to where you are. Like unusual landforms, they can help a child figure out where he is. "The beargrass was all bloomed out down where we started our hike; we've been climbing higher and here it's just coming out. . . . This forest is so shady, all that seems to grow under the trees is ferns. . . . See how the branches on all these trees are skimpy on one side and full on the other? The wind causes that."

As kids get along in years they should be reminded to think of a wild place in terms of the overall shape and features of the land. **Every detail they are encouraged to notice is a potential clue for staying found.** Learn (perhaps along with them) something of the geology of the region. Did glaciers carve this valley? Why is this headwall so steep and not eroded to a smooth and gentle slope? Was that line of rock rubble pushed off the mountain by a glacier? How did this cone-shaped pile of rocks form? Why is this meadow treeless, when the one we just passed had little pines growing in the lower end? How many colors can you find in the cliff face near camp?

Continuously give kids a progress report on where your group is and where it's going: "At the trail fork just around the next bend, we'll be halfway to camp . . . the next mile is all downhill. Then we'll have lunch where the trail crosses Windigo Creek. . . . There's a fork where a side trail comes down from Aspen Butte. We stay left."

Give older kids a turn at leading the group, with careful instructions not to get way ahead of the pack and to regroup at every junction, and maybe at the beginnings of steep stretches. Gently tutor the young scout in observing landmarks as they come into view and in frequently looking over his shoulder for a backward perspective. Before a youngster takes the lead, trace your route on the map with him, teaching the rudiments of map-reading a tiny bit at a time as you do so.

When you get to camp, take the kids in hand for a visual inventory of the surroundings. Direct their attention in particular to landmarks that stand out and could be seen by one who wandered away and got confused about how to get back. "See that cliff with the scraggly trees on top? That's right behind camp. . . . The only waterfall the map shows on this stream is *upstream* from

camp, not far. . . . If you drew a line between that big mountain with snow on top and the lower one that's all reddish and bare, it would go right through our camp."

In the middle elementary grades kids are old enough to start learning the language of topographic maps. If you begin to introduce the simplest elements of this skill when kids are quite young, they'll be masters before they reach their teens. As with any area of learning, be careful not to turn beginners off by smothering them in too much information at one time.

Explain contour lines, the basic feature of a topographic map, with the aid of a pond and a lumpy rock. The pond is "sea level" and the rock "a hill." Dip part of the rock into the water, then mark the waterline with pen or pencil. Make a parallel "higher elevation contour line" by dipping the rock deeper and marking the new waterline. With your child, trace these lines over the rock's surface, showing how each line marks a given elevation above "sea level" whether it goes across a smooth part of the rock, around a bulge or into a dent. Now graduate to a nearby hill and compare it with its map picture.

At rest stops and quiet times in camp, play guessing games with your map.

■ Start with the simplest symbols: How many streams can you find? Where is a swampy place? Is there more forest or open land?

■ Move on to more advanced concepts: Which mountain is tallest? Can you find a hill with an unwooded east side? Will we hike *up* or *down* this steep part of the trail tomorrow? Here's where we are now. What mountain is about a mile ahead in the same direction we've been hiking?

■ As your kids' map-reading fluency progresses they'll be ready to tackle harder questions: Does this stream flow into or out of Frying Pan Lake? How much elevation will we gain between camp and the junction with Horseshoe Trail? Can you find a good campsite about a day's hike north? Where would you put it if you were going to make a trail between Sunrise Lake and Marmot Pass, and why did you pick that route?

By this stage, they'll be firing questions in your direction.

At about the same time as you introduce maps, begin teaching the most basic compass operations. Kids love gadgets! Magnetic declination won't make sense for quite a while, but there are many things a hiker can do with compass alone, without adjusting for declination.

The main idea in these early years is to get familiar with the compass, its parts, the notion that a circle is divided into 360 degrees, and how to take and follow simple bearings. Then, as a youngster learns to use topographic maps, he'll eventually be able to put the two together. Even if his compass skills extend no farther than orienting the map (which can be rote-learned before one understands declination), that single ability could help him stay found.

Kids thoroughly enjoy finding north by their noontime shadow, with the stick-shadow routine, and in the night sky with the Big and Little Dippers.

As the trail years with your family go by, encourage any budding interest kids show in route-finding by giving them compasses and maps of their own. Maps showing country they've hiked themselves will seem special to them.

Key Ways to Help Kids

Top priority: What to do if you feel lost.

Other aids, in ascending order for age and ability level. Adapt each to your child's readiness and needs.

1. Insist on two rules: Let others know where you are. Stay within camp activity boundaries.

2. Explain how to get back to camp when it's out of sight.

3. Help your child notice details wherever he travels (constant awareness).

4. Teach how to recognize a trail.

5. Give a continuous progress report as your group hikes.

6. Teach how to lead on the trail.

7. Teach the basics of map-reading.

8. Show how to use a compass.

11

Route-finding on Snow

We'd been skiing for four days since our last food pickup and contact with civilization, three fourths of the way into a snow journey through Oregon's Cascades. It was demanding country for finding one's way—a couple of big peaks, when we could see them; jumbled lower hills and dozens of little lakes set in thick fir and hemlock forests. The day before, we had strayed too far west into an area filled with springs which undercut the snow and called for tense corrective maneuvers. This day we had a good ongoing notion of where we were, having identified several larger lakes. Still, when we set up camp it was recorded with a tentative "X?" on the map. Reconnaissance probes after dinner located us right at map's edge, since nothing to the west matched any patterns on our paper guide.

You can find solitude, adventure and beauty in the white seasons without going far, by making use of unplowed roads that are easy to get to. But finding your way

around the winter landscape is usually far from simple. The minute you ski away from the prepared track, you *must* be a skilled route-finder.

Picture a trail brushed out to a height of eight feet. Now put a four-foot snowpack on that trail. The cleared tunnel through the trees is now only chest-high and not nearly so obvious. To confuse matters more, you can see several other cleared places that could be the trail.

With trails and signs covered and blazes usually unrecognizable, the land itself is more your guide. But visibility is predictably poorer in winter, so it's often difficult to see landmarks at much distance. Like the cross-country summer traveler, the snowgoer must be constantly aware of his location in the wider landscape and conscious of the direction he's moving. But he must be even more self-reliant, able to handle the greater logistical problems of getting from here to there on a tricky, changeable ground cover—and skis are a bit harder to handle than legs. And the consequences of route-finding errors are potentially much more serious.

If finding your way around on snow is so much more work, why do it? Well, *that's* partly why—the challenge and satisfaction. And remember wanting to avoid crowds in the wilderness? Going in winter is a sure way, once you're out of sight of the parking lot.

What's Different about Winter Wandering?

It's a whole new world out there. Besides the usual lack of trail and sign guidelines and generally poorer visibility, many other factors affect the winter navigator:

- His route and campsite choices are virtually limitless. He can often move right over brushy tangles that thwart hikers, and camp in meadows and on lakeshores without damaging the land.

- Because days are shorter and camp routines more time-consuming, there's usually less travel time.

- Some kinds of terrain take less energy to negotiate. Unless he falls a lot, going downhill is a skier's free ride.

- Some things can be harder work. Going up a steep hillside usually takes more energy, what with kick-turns and all.

- The pace of snow travel is much more variable. It depends on more than just how much elevation is gained or lost in a mile, or how well the trail is maintained.

- Several terrain hazards are peculiar to

winter: tree wells, cornices, avalanche slopes, icy or crusty snow, bad ice on lakes.

■ Water crossings can be much trickier and can take more time.

■ Deciphering the landscape is frequently difficult. A flat open area could be a lake, meadow or swamp. Drifts can hide small streams and make them look like snow-filled gullies.

■ Good depth perception and an accurate assessment of distance are hard to come by when snow covers everything, and even harder with overcast skies.

Planning a Snow Trip

Until you've been out several times and feel friendly with the logistics of winter travel, keep your trips easy, conservative, close to help. Aim for the *least* mileage you could make in a day with poor conditions and use the slack, if any, for play. Plan to reach the day's destination at least two hours before dark. In December that could mean stopping as early as three o'clock.

Until you're there, it's very difficult to judge how much time it will take to cover a given piece of terrain. A heavy dumping of new powder snow or a warming trend can make even road-skiing tediously slow. Some mornings you may find the snow so icy that it's simply unskiable for a couple of hours, but walking on it doesn't work either. Since temperatures and snow conditions are so variable and unpredictable, your route plan should be both conservative and flexible. If it isn't, you may pressure yourself into some bad decisions just to stick to the plan.

Learn all you can from map study at home so you can choose a route that avoids foreseeable hazards such as avalanche slopes. Any steep open slope should be suspect. Sometimes the map will alert you by strips of white in larger green areas, marking where avalanches have wiped out the tree cover. Don't plan to rely on visual guides such as small streams or distant ridges, since both can disappear.

Pick terrain that's basically hospitable—gentle slopes, some open areas, distinctive terrain features, not too many problematic water crossings. Locate a base line or two, and note how far you'd have to go for help or to evacuate one of your number, and in what direction. Lay out some alternate routes which could be used if needed. Is there a power-line cut or logging road you could use to reduce travel distance, should the weather deteriorate?

Often you'll deliberately avoid trying to follow a trail laid out for hikers. These trails tend to make frequent ups and downs, detour to scenic waterfalls, and cross high, steep areas for their great views. Such scenery is lovely, but not hospitable to snow travelers. You might plan a route that is near a hiking trail but hangs farther back from stream banks, whose undercut cornices can break away, or skirts the edge of a lake basin instead of threading through it.

Planning a snow trip, you need to pay closer attention to water crossings, since you can't simply wade across; you might *have* to sometime, as a last resort, but this chilling experience is best avoided. If your route takes in both sides of a sizable stream, it may be essential that you find the one bridge over it, even though you don't want to be on the trail the rest of the time. If a stream is too wide to step across and doesn't have a sturdy snow bridge, you may spend considerable time locating a workable log crossing and negotiating it when you do.

Noting the availability of water along your route is important. Yes, you can always melt snow to meet your liquid intake needs, but it's a lot easier and quicker if you don't have to. Especially in very cold weather, try to camp near a water source.

If your snow trip is in areas laced with logging roads, be *sure* you supplement your USGS topographic map with the most recent Forest Service or Bureau of Land Management map showing roads. The snowpack may cover signs and road numbers, but such a map will still do a lot to lessen your confusion.

Get as much advance information as possible about the area from others who've been there, outdoor stores, nearby resorts, the agency in charge of the land. These sources can fill in the picture with things a map can't tell you, such as the direction of the prevailing winds (which determine where cornices build up on exposed ridges), the snow depth and which lakes are frozen over.

You might want to preplot your route and bearings at home, where your warm fingers work better. And be sure to protect your maps from the debilitating damp before you head out.

On the Move

Keep map, compass, paper and pencil handy so you can make constant notes on your progress. Some people check off landmarks as they are passed. In general, follow all the rules that apply to cross-country travel, but with even greater care. If you keep good track of where you are, then a sudden reduction of visibility or mismatch of map and landscape won't cause panic. You'll be able to think back just a few minutes to when things did make sense.

Many snow travelers grow careless about route-finding, taking comfort in the idea that they can always follow their own tracks back to where they came from. This might work, but don't count on it. Just a few minutes of blowing snow can obliterate those tracks. And it's possible to confuse your tracks with those of others in the area. Depending on the snow and weather conditions, it's also sometimes difficult to distinguish between today's tracks (yours) and yesterday's (someone else's).

Habitually make use of all available route-finding clues. Keenly observe terrain features both large and small. Pay constant attention to the weather so you won't miss any brief moments of clearing. Fast-moving clouds may bare a crucial landmark just long enough for you to take a compass bearing on it. Refer continually to the map.

By noticing *many* distinguishing features about your route and goals, you can avoid a lot of energy-wasting stumbling around. Are you headed for a meadow at the foot of a large peak? Look around and on the map for other clues about the area: a notch in the north spur ridge is above the border of the meadow; there's a stream flowing toward you from the other edge; between you and the clearing, the land makes a gentle rise between two east-west draws.

Now, once you start out for the meadow, you have several clues to keep you on course. Even if the tall peak disappears as your perspective changes, you might see

the spur ridge, whose notch will tell you if you've come too far north. So would the draw on that side. And if you hit the stream on the left, you'll know to follow it to the meadow's south border.

Since you aren't bound to, or lulled by, a trail in winter, a feeling for the total landscape is both essential and inescapable. On a summer trail hike you may round the shoulder of a hill and hardly be aware of what you're doing. In winter, you make a deliberate choice to cover the country along certain routes.

Some terrain features present special problems. Streams may be hard to identify. You can ski right over a frozen creek without realizing it, or be convinced that an empty gully is a frozen creek. A lovely "meadow" may be a lake in white disguise, or vice versa. The *shape* of an open expanse may be the clue that leads to positive identification. Areas of deciduous trees that were green in summer—and still are, on the map—are now just bare sticks against a white background. You may have laid out a route through a treed area, only to find the woods too dense to get through.

If the map indicates a swamp but it's covered with a good snowpack, it could still be unsafe to travel across. Decaying vegetation creates heat that melts the supportive snow from underneath. This kind of undercutting can also happen around springs, near beaver and muskrat houses, and where streams enter and leave lakes. Stream banks and snow bridges should always be respected for the possibility of undercutting.

The combination of weather and terrain can affect route choice. Plan stream crossings on snow bridges for the cool morning hours, when they're still firmly frozen. A sudden warming trend and rain can swell tiny step-across creeks to raging torrents in a matter of hours.

Ridges between stream beds can sometimes provide good passage. There's less tangled brush, no avalanche danger, and frequently a better view of landmarks. But if the ridge is exposed and the day stormy, that's not the place to be. Steep open slopes that spell avalanche danger sometimes call for wide detours. So do ridges with built-up cornices ready to let go on travelers underneath. You may have planned to ski across a lake that has suddenly started to thaw. Or perhaps the snow is just too icy on open shoulders along your planned route.

Any of the above situations could call for a deviation from your plan. When that happens, choose the easiest, most efficient way around, which is often not the shortest. If you have to deviate from the planned route to get around the obstacles, measure the deviation by time and your speed of travel, and compensate back as soon as possible. If you've detoured twenty minutes to the west to get around a brushy area, you'll need to reverse not only direction, but the same twenty minutes to find the draw you were following. Be sure to keep track of things *as they happen* rather than in retrospect.

Be extremely cautious about traveling in poor visibility. Not only is it easier to get lost or hurt . . . it isn't as much fun.

Full of stimulating challenges, winter route-finding will convince you that there's always more to learn.

ABOUT THE AUTHOR

JUNE FLEMING, who lives in Portland, Oregon, has backpacked the length of Oregon and made hundreds of snow-camping trips in the Cascades mountain range.